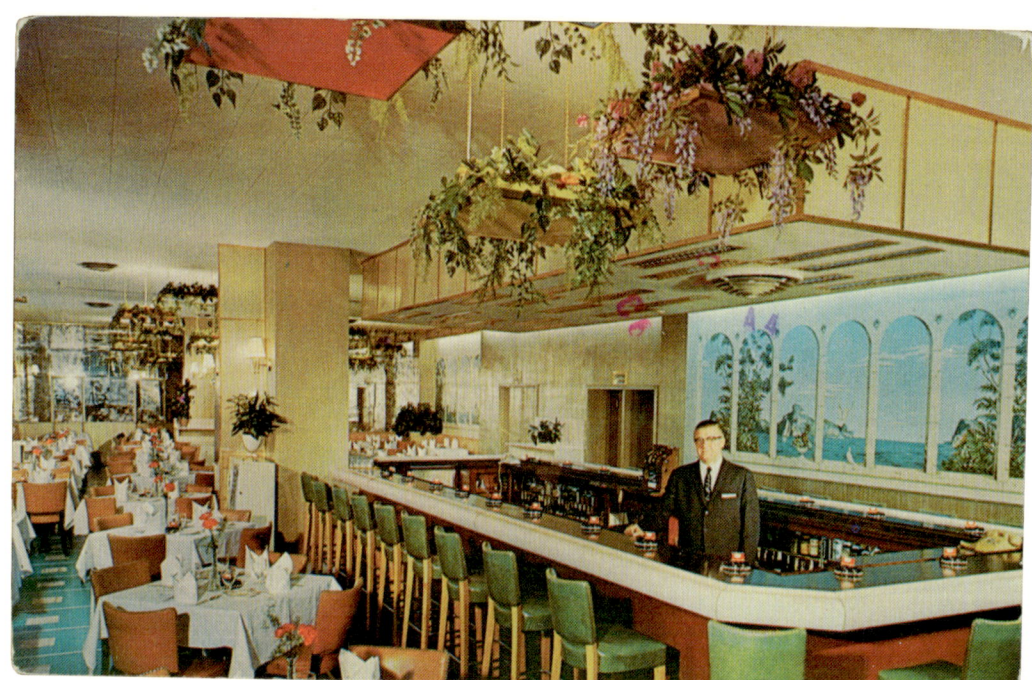

aperture

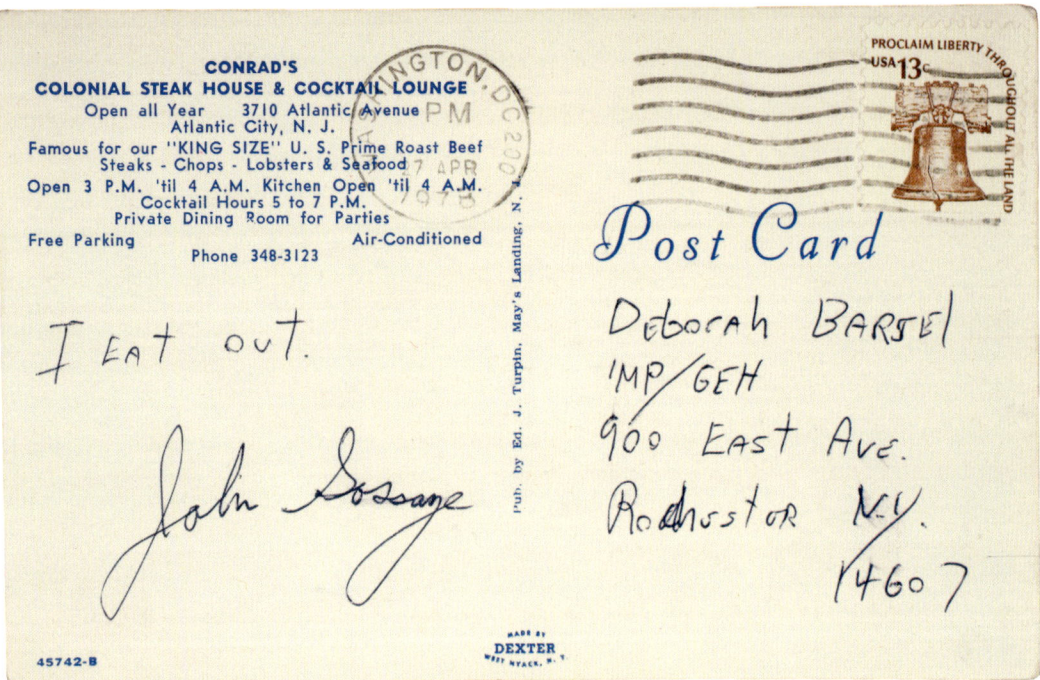

CONRAD'S
COLONIAL STEAK HOUSE & COCKTAIL LOUNGE
Open all Year   3710 Atlantic Avenue
Atlantic City, N. J.
Famous for our "KING SIZE" U. S. Prime Roast Beef
Steaks - Chops - Lobsters & Seafood
Open 3 P.M. 'til 4 A.M. Kitchen Open 'til 4 A.M.
Cocktail Hours 5 to 7 P.M.
Private Dining Room for Parties
Free Parking   Air-Conditioned
Phone 348-3123

I EAT out.

John Gossage

PROCLAIM LIBERTY THROUGHOUT ALL THE LAND

USA 13c

Post Card

Deborah BARTEl
IMP/GEH
900 East Ave.
Rochester N.Y.
14607

45742-B

MADE BY
DEXTER
WEST NYACK, N. Y.

Postcard from John Gossage, submitted to
The Photographer's Cookbook, 1978

The Photographer's Cookbook

Originally conceived
and edited by Deborah Barsel

Introduction
by Lisa Hostetler

Contents

Main Dishes

Vegetables

Breads & Starches

Desserts

Drinks

Food
for Thought

Lisa
Hostetler

It was 1977, and Deborah Barsel, assistant registrar at George Eastman House (as the George Eastman Museum was then known), struck upon the idea of compiling a book of photographers' recipes. She was bored in her job and wanted to take on a fun extracurricular project. With the support of her supervisor, Andrew Eskind, she placed a notice in the museum's magazine, Image, requesting submissions of photographers' favorite recipes and food-related photographs. She also wrote letters to photographers inviting them to participate in the project, and to her surprise, many of them wrote back. A couple of years later, she had over 120 responses and began organizing them for publication. Unfortunately, Barsel left the museum to enroll in graduate school before the book was complete, and her planned cookbook never came to fruition.

Over thirty-five years later, a box labeled "Photo Cookbook" came to my attention shortly after I arrived at the museum. When I opened the box, I found neatly organized files of Barsel's correspondence, along with materials and recipes she had gathered for the book. There was a handwritten letter from Brassaï apologizing for missing the deadline for submission and expressing his hope that his photograph and recipe could still be included; a recipe for two classic Southern dishes from William Eggleston; instructions for making and enjoying Robert Heinecken's favorite martini ("not recommended before 11:00 a.m."); Ansel Adams's recipe for poached eggs in beer; and a postcard from John Gossage stating, "I eat out," among many other submissions. Many of the photographs provided for the cookbook were still in the museum's vault (although some had also been returned long ago). I was thrilled and intrigued, and so was Aperture's senior editor Denise Wolff, who had heard about the project and came to Rochester to see if something might be done with it.

We agreed that something could, and should be done, and you are holding the results of our efforts in your hands.

The Photographer's Cookbook is a virtual time capsule of the photography community in the 1970s. Famous masters of the medium such as Ansel Adams, whose iconic black-and-white landscapes were synonymous with the emerging market for art photography at the time, are here, but so are William Eggleston and Stephen Shore, young upstarts whose work was just beginning to draw the attention of the contemporary art world. Other photographers who contributed to this recipe collection worked not only in the realm of art but also fashion (Richard Avedon and Horst P. Horst), advertising (Ralph Steiner), and photojournalism (Burt Glinn). Some of their recipes and photographs were submitted with a wink and a nod, such as Neal Slavin's motley squad of hot dogs in "full dress," as well as conceptual-art fascinations like Les Krims's "Formalist Stew." The first wave of the alternative-process revival is represented here as well, with entries by Betty Hahn and Bea Nettles. And the inclusion of Robert Heinecken and Jerry Uelsmann demonstrated a refreshing embrace of non-"straight" photography, unusual for the time. Some of the photographers included here are less known today than they were when the cookbook was conceived, but their recipes and images are nevertheless novel and timely, such as Joseph Jachna's "Potato Chip Cookies."

It makes sense that this recipe and photograph collection originated at the Eastman Museum. After all, George Eastman was known to have enjoyed cooking. He did most of his cooking while hunting or on safari, with a few exceptions. One dish he made regularly while at home was lemon meringue pie, which he baked for friends on special occasions. He even challenged one friend, Edwin Ingersoll, to a pie-making contest (Eastman won). When he built his Rochester, New York, mansion, he designed a combination kitchen/laboratory on the third floor, a feature of the house that his cook Eliza especially appreciated, given Eastman's tendency to meddle in the cooking that happened in the regular kitchen. The Eastman Museum had another famous "foodie in residence," its first curator and long-time director Beaumont Newhall. Newhall's knowledge and interest in cooking almost matched his expertise in photography's history. From 1956 to 1969 he wrote a cooking column for the Brighton-Pittsford Post (Brighton and Pittsford are suburbs of Rochester) called the "Epicure Corner," and his reputation as a cook and gourmet was well documented by members of his circle in Santa Fe where he moved after his tenure at the museum ended in 1971. His recipe for "Choucroute" (a cabbage and meat dish), along with his story about how he served it to the famous chef James Beard, is also included in this collection.

There is a close relationship between photography and cooking that extends well beyond the interests of these two titans of photographic history, however. Before the advent of the digital age, many amateur and professional photographers spent hours in the darkroom making and mixing chemicals to concoct variations (their own recipes, if you will) on standard photochemical procedures to suit their aesthetic impulses. In another sense, photography itself can be understood in terms of cooking and alchemy; both chefs and photographers regularly transmute ordinary matter into works of great value and rarity. Whether the pleasure of consuming them is visual or alimentary, creativity is critical to successful results.

In addition, reading (and cooking) a photographer's favorite recipe gives us insight into that individual's personality, tastes, and background. The fact that Robert Adams loves home-baked sugar cookies and that Ed Ruscha enjoys a Southwestern staple like the cactus omelette is not surprising, but it is telling.

Such details cast their subjects in familiar terms, and the recipes thus bring the reader and cook closer to the photographers and their art. Everyone has likes and dislikes when it comes to food, and these preferences are unassailable—that is, few consider an aversion to beets to be a moral flaw. In this respect, the sharing of favorite recipes can be a great humanizer.

A recipe can also be a bellwether of cultural currency. To review these recipes is to visit a time when the perils of cholesterol and saturated fat had yet to be fully understood, a time when recipes calling for Velveeta and lard were not unusual. As a child of the 1970s who found confusing the simultaneous advocacy of "natural" living, fast food, and TV dinners in the era's popular culture, I find it somehow comforting that the photographers whose work I admire for their visual sophistication were dining on both hot dogs and cheesecake. On the other side of the coin, Linda Connor's "Pumpkin-Pomegranate Soup" sounds deliciously contemporary, and Minor White's "Steamed and Sautéed Vegetables" is a reminder that wholesome food, prepared simply, is as timeless as the Zen Buddhism that infused everything White did.

In the end, Wolff and I edited the contents of Barsel's "Photo Cookbook" box down to about fifty recipes and pictures that best summarize the contemporary significance of the project. We've retained the chapters originally intended for the book and kept the recipes as-is, except in rare cases when there was a clear mistake or omission. You may try cooking one of these recipes in your own kitchen, or you may prefer instead just to peruse the pictures and recipes, engaging with those artists who shaped the photography community upon which the current one is built. Either way, The Photographer's Cookbook will provide you with a valuable artistic and culinary experience— not to mention a great deal of fun. Bon appétit.

Breakfast Foods

Ansel Adams's Eggs Poached in Beer

¼ cup (2 ounces) butter
Mixed spices
1 bottle dark malt liquor or
    strong ale (ordinary beer
    is not strong enough)

Dash sherry
¼ teaspoon salt
2 eggs
2 pieces toast
Dash paprika

1) Melt butter in microwave oven, but do not allow to brown. Add a dash of mixed spices and sherry.

2) In a small bowl, microwave malt or ale with ¼ teaspoon salt just to the boiling point. Carefully slide eggs into this hot liquid, cover with paper plate or glass bowl (to retain thermal heat), and cook as desired in microwave. (See note below on microwave cooking.)

3) While eggs are cooking in microwave, make 2 pieces of toast. Spread part of the butter-spice mix over the toast.

4) Serve eggs on the toast, and pour over the rest of the butter-spice mix. Add a dash of paprika.

Note on microwave cooking:
I like my eggs poached soft. I find that 1 egg in the hot ale or malt takes about 1 minute to cook, 2 eggs about 2 minutes, etc., all the way up to 8 eggs about 8 minutes. When working with as many as 8 eggs, the bowl should be moved around every 2–3 minutes.

14 Ansel Adams, Still Life, San Francisco,
    1932

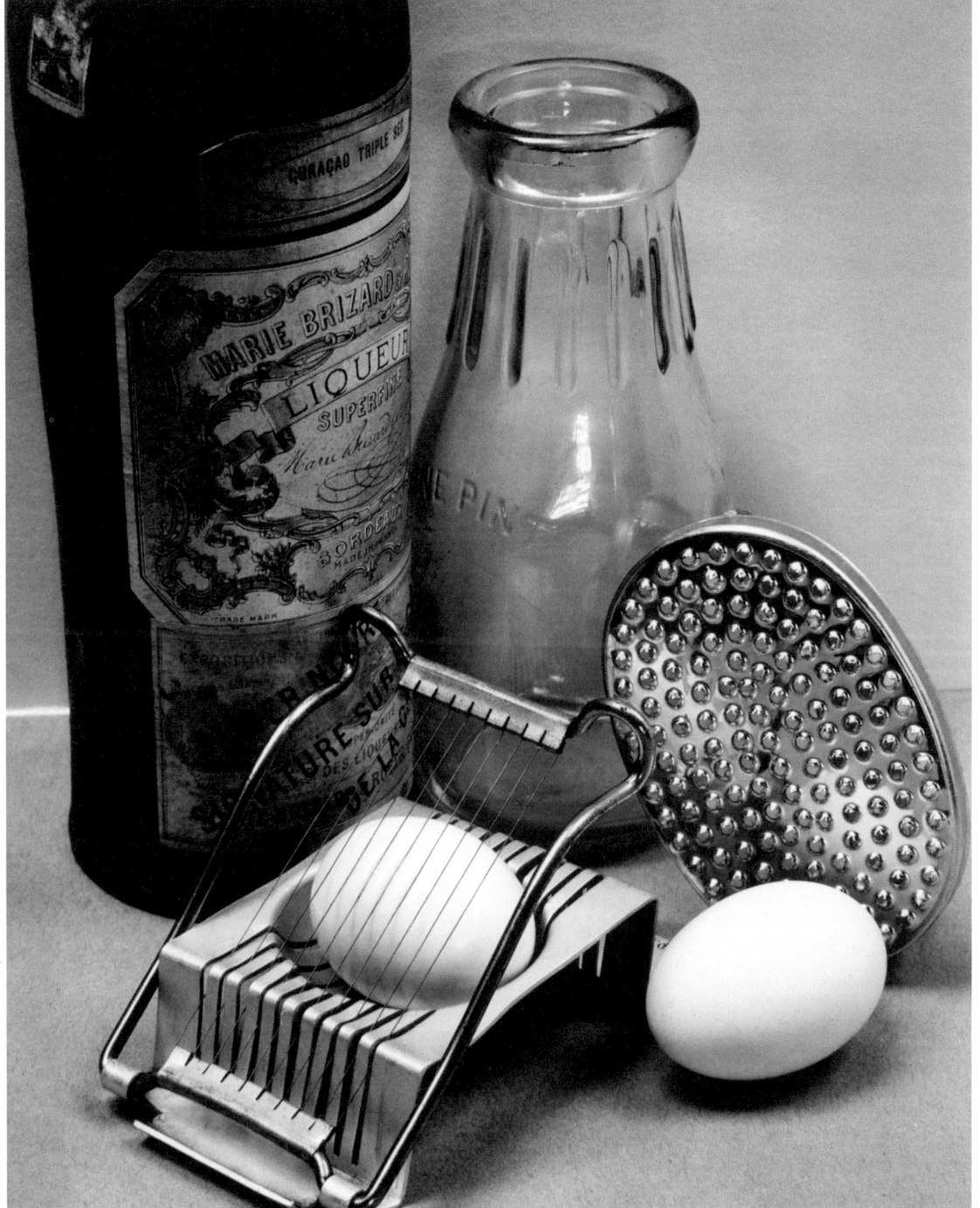

Brassaï's Du Lard Paprikas Hongrois (Hungarian Pork Belly Spread)

1) Choose a handsome piece of pork belly with no trace
    of meat on it. Cut into long square pieces and attach string
    to each piece for hanging.

2) Stick each piece of pork belly with at least 10 cloves
    of garlic.

3) Boil water in a large pot. When water is boiling, throw
    in the pieces of pork belly, and boil for 12 minutes. They
    will become translucent.

4) On a towel, sprinkle a good layer of Hungarian paprika
    (or paprika from another country). After draining the
    pieces of pork belly and removing the garlic cloves, roll
    each piece in paprika until it becomes red all over.

5) Now, you just have to hang the pieces of pork belly on nails
    using the string. It keeps for a few months.

Du Lard Paprikas Hongrois is eaten with coffee or milk
at breakfast, cutting it into very thin slices and spreading
it on bread. A bit like eating bread with butter.

16   Brassaï, Au Cochon Limousin,
      1935

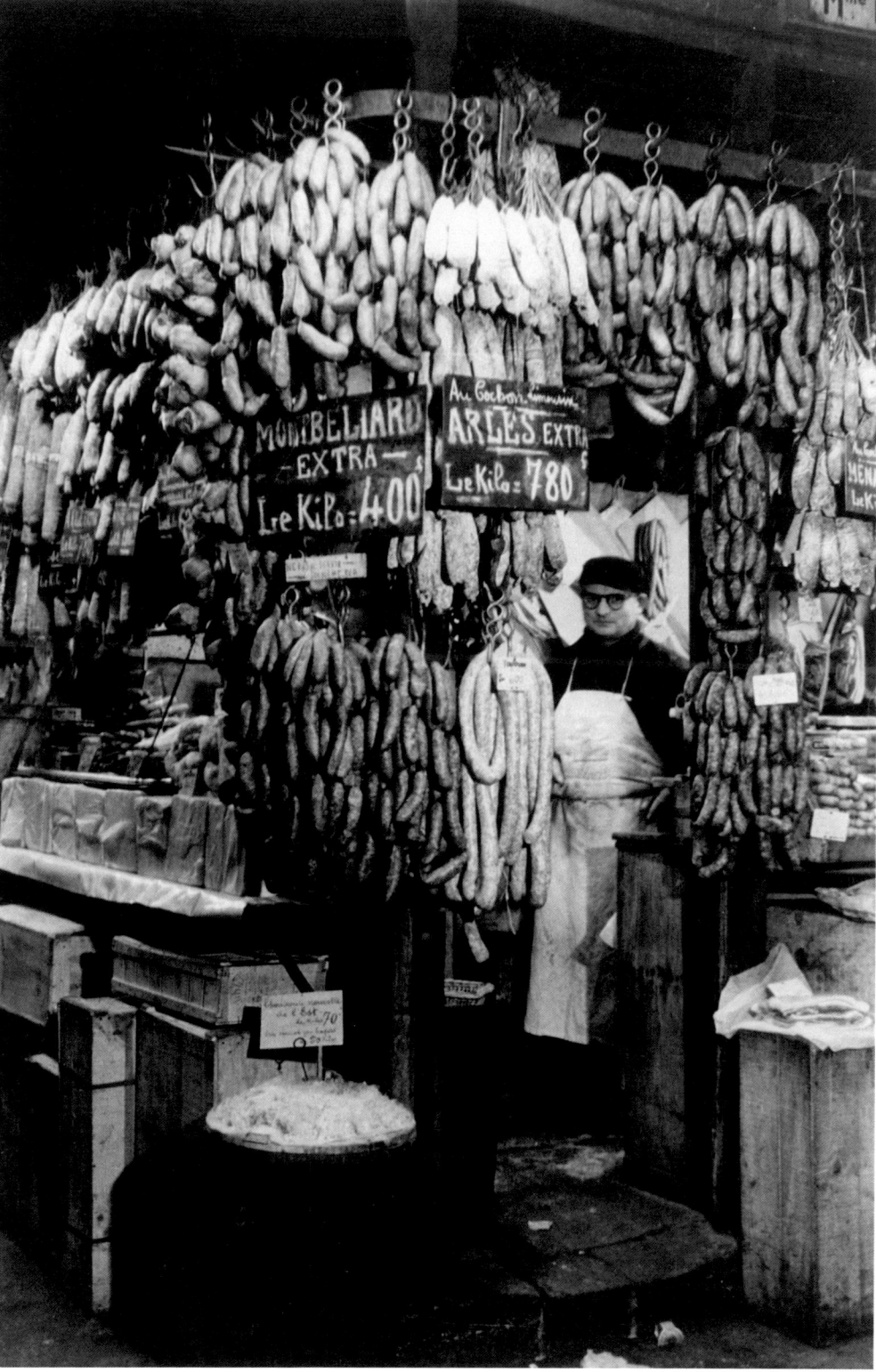

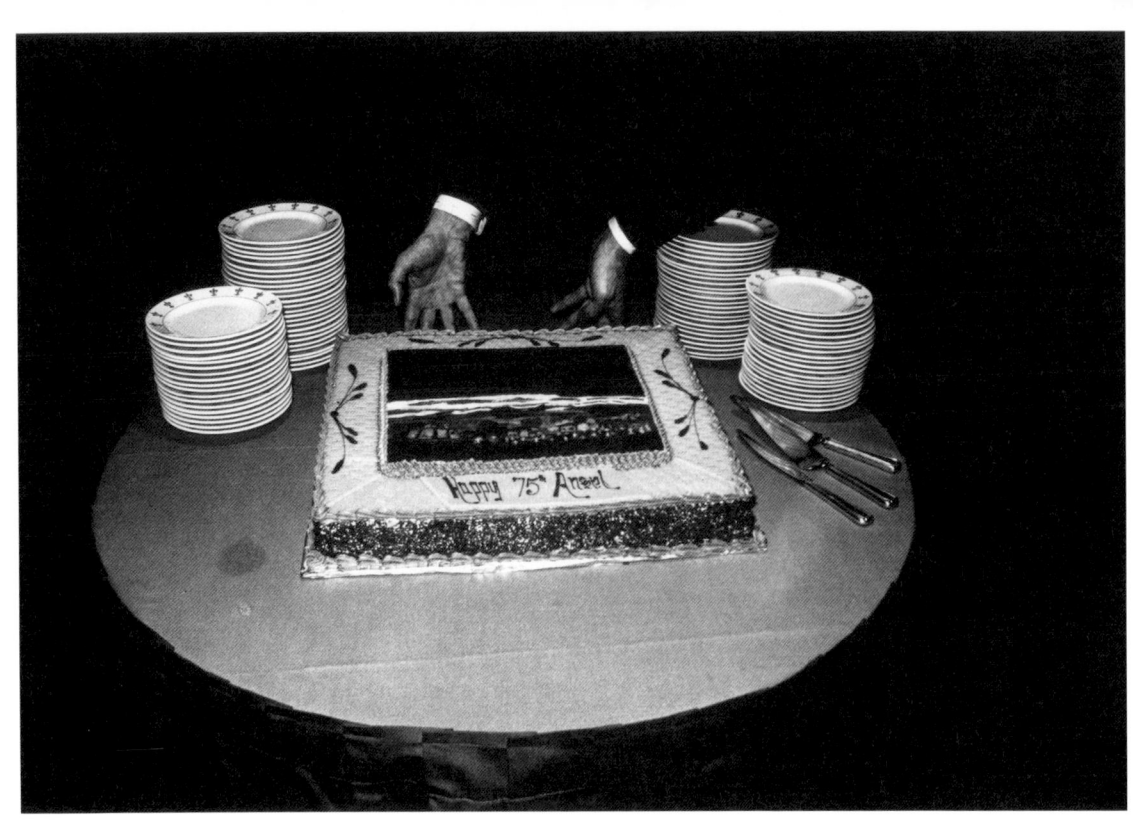

18   Judy Dater, <u>Ansel's 75th Birthday Cake</u>
<u>with John Szarkowski's Hands</u>, 1977

Judy Dater's Tortillas and Eggs

Here is one of my favorite breakfast recipes. It is a California/Mexico-inspired dish, just right for a Sunday brunch.

Sauté ½ green pepper, ¼ pound mushrooms, and several green onions, all chopped, in lots of butter. Add 4 to 6 beaten eggs, and stir until cooked. While eggs are cooking, steam several flour or corn tortillas. I use a Chinese wok and vegetable steamer. Have 1 ripe tomato chopped, 1 avocado chopped, some prepared hot sauce of your choice, and lots of shredded cheddar cheese ready. When tortillas are steamed and eggs are cooked, roll the tortillas with egg, tomatoes, avocado, cheese, and add hot sauce to taste.

For an extra treat, have a large pitcher of margaritas to go with the concoction.

William Eggleston's Cheese Grits Casserole

1 cup grits	⅓ cup milk
1 teaspoon salt	½ pound Velveeta
4 cups water	cheese
1 stick butter	3 eggs, slightly beaten

Cook as usual grits in salted water until done. Then add butter, cheese, eggs, and milk. Stir until melted smooth. Place in quart casserole, and bake for 1 hour at 350 degrees.

Serves 6–8.

19   William Eggleston, Untitled,
      1976; from the series Election Eve

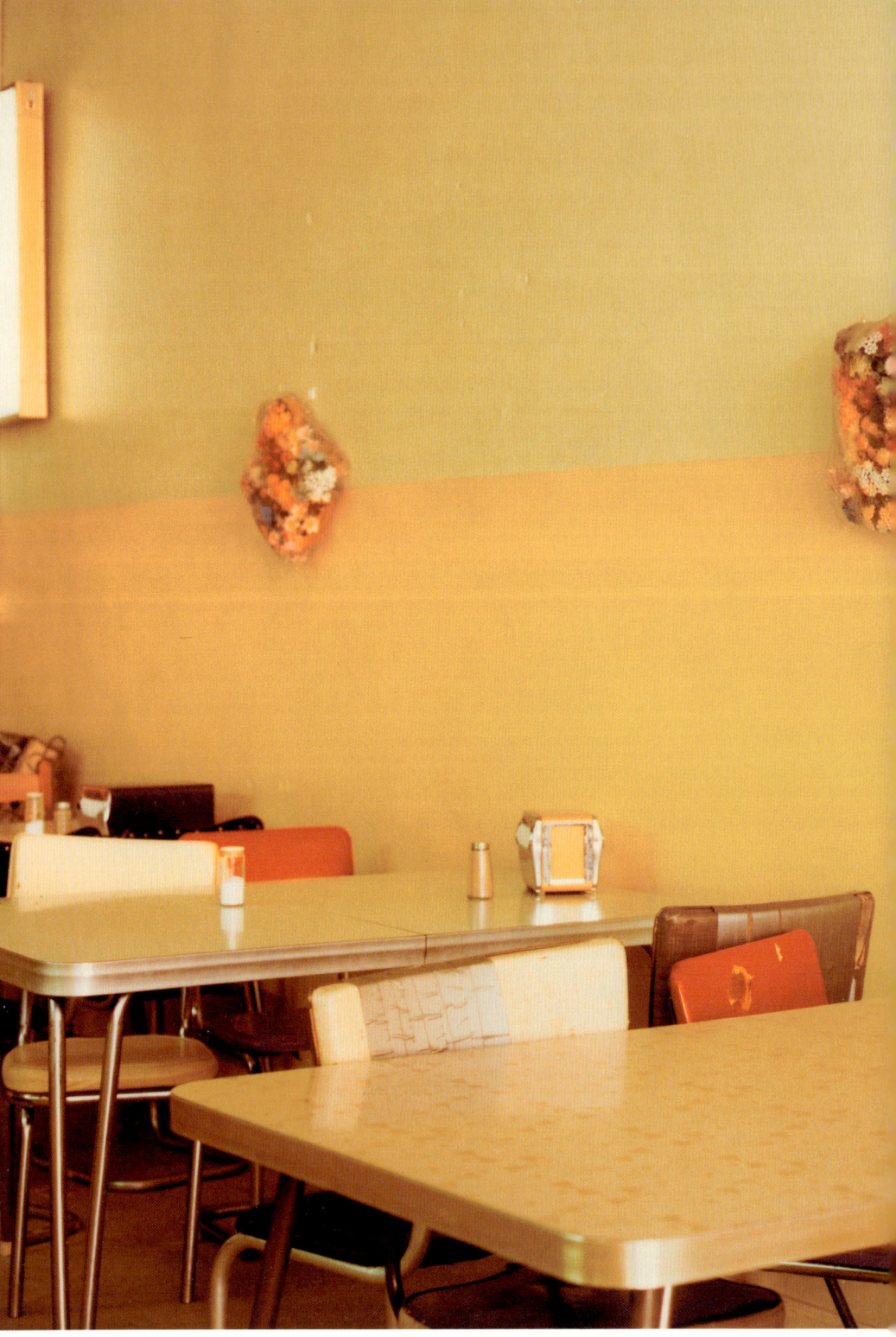

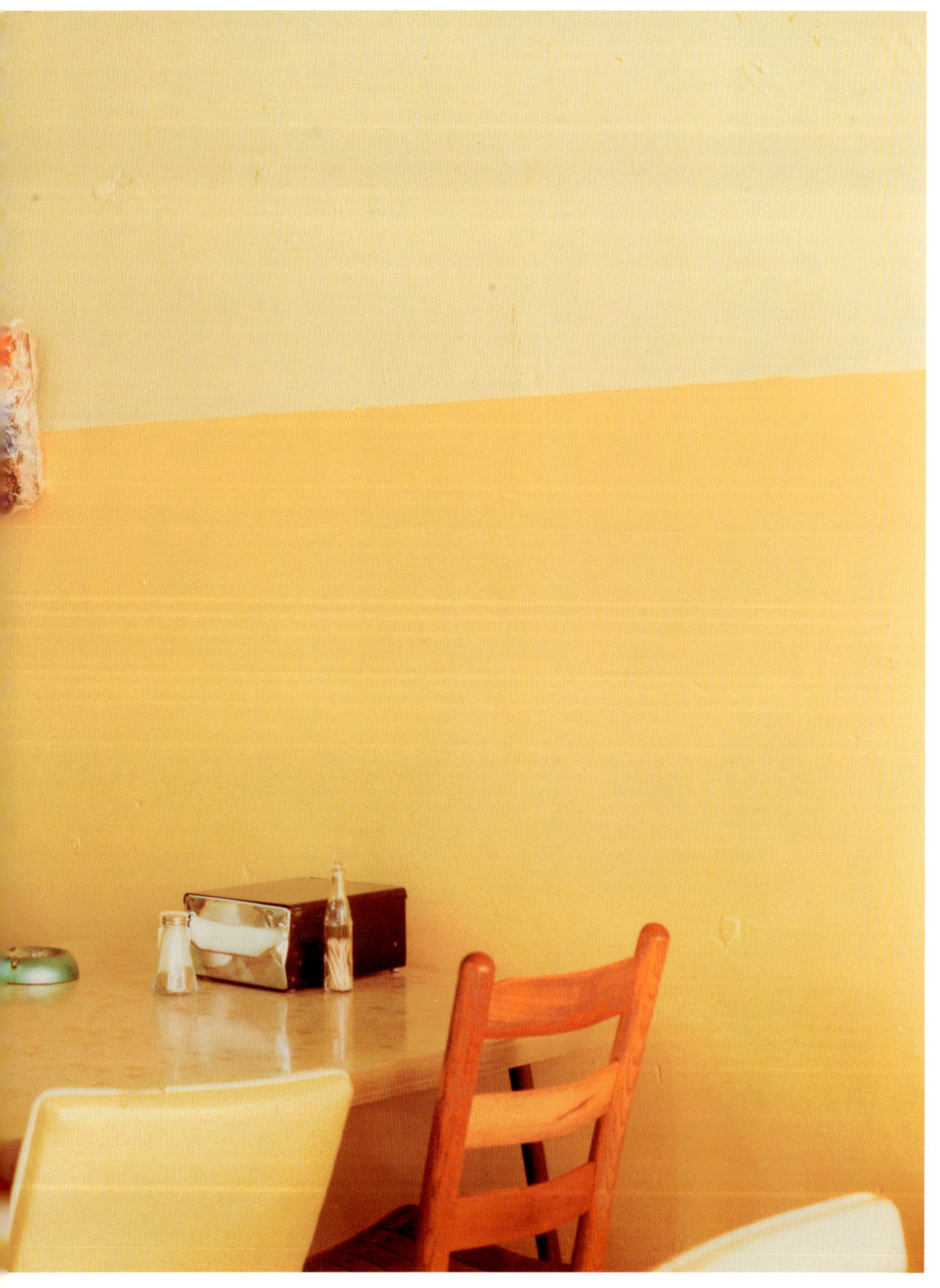

Ed Ruscha's Cactus Omelette

Ingredients

    2 eggs from any farm

    1 tablespoon sweet butter

    2 tablespoons small curd cottage cheese

    2 tablespoons diced celery

    3 tablespoons nopalitos (diced cactus)—available at most
        grocers on the West Coast, have a friend bring a jar
        on a plane, if necessary

    Salt

    Pepper

Utensils

    Omelette pan or similar type of pan with rounded bottom

    Mixing bowl

    Wire whisk or fork

Instructions

    Break eggs into a bowl. Slightly under-mix with whisk
or fork. Heat butter in pan until it bubbles and begins to
turn brown. Add eggs, and let them sit in pan until bottom
begins to harden. At this point, lift the edges ever so
slightly so that the runny top layer can slip under on all
sides. As soon as this sets, but while the top is still moist,
add the cottage cheese in a line down the center, as you
will be folding the omelette in half. Sprinkle the diced
celery on top of the cottage cheese, followed by the
nopalitos. Fold the empty side over so that it produces
a half-circle. Let the omelette set for about 1 minute
on low fire. Roll omelette out of the pan and onto the plate.
Salt. Pepper. It's yours.

22   Ed Ruscha, from the series Colored People,
      1972

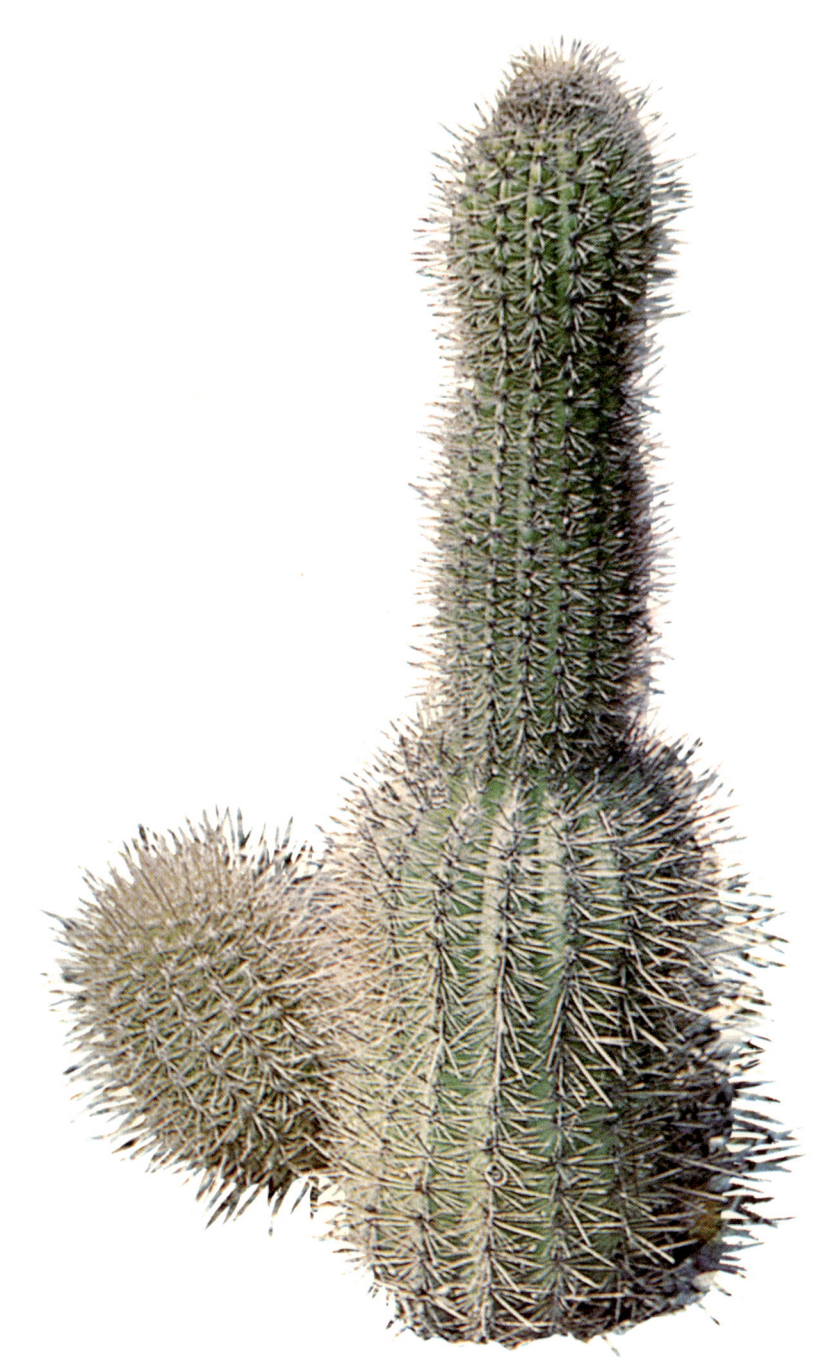

Ralph Steiner's Zwei Vier Minuten Eier

Basically I am more a basse cuisine than a haute cuisine chef.
I got my Cordon Bleu not in Paris but in Erie, Pennsylvania.
There I learned two accomplishments:

a.   How to take a box of cornflakes down from the shelf.
b.   How to boil 2 four-minute eggs.

Eggs are important! You, of course, recall Samuel Butler's
famous solution of the ancient question: "Which came first, the
chicken or the egg?" He said: "The egg came first: a chicken is
only an egg's way of making another egg."

Now for my favorite/only recipe:

One puts water an egg's diameter deep into a pan. Turns heat on.
When boiling briskly, drops 2 eggs in from low altitude. Turns
heat off. One watches one's watch watchfully for 240 seconds.
At the stroke of 240, one removes eggs. On opening eggs I always
manage to get some bits of shell—or is it "will"—in my eggs.
I never know when to use "shell" and when to use "will." Never
mind; a bit of shell ingested gives a man shell power.

24   Ralph Steiner, Ham and Eggs,
     advertisement for the Delineator, 1929

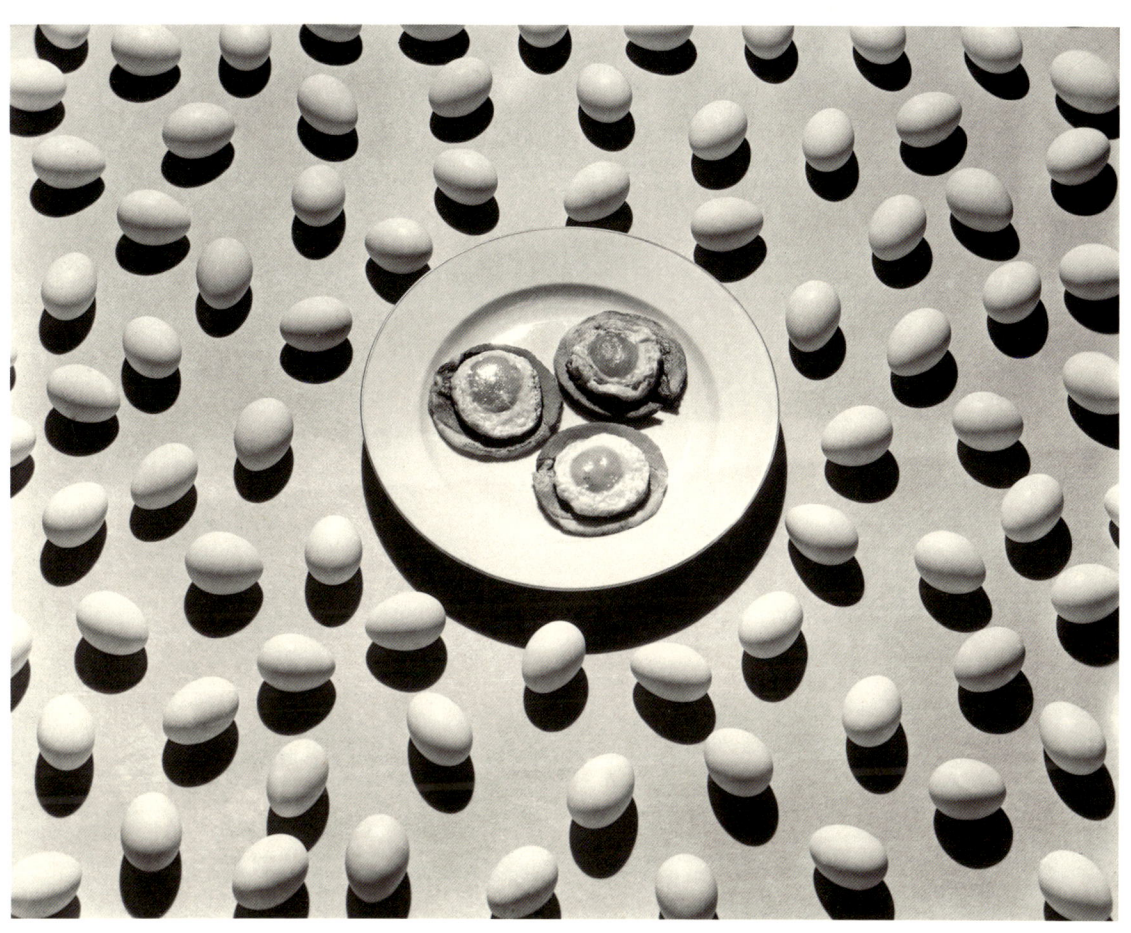

Fast Foods
& Appetizers

Bill Arnold's The Melted Cheese Sandwich

I like a fast couple of sandwiches. I'll pretty much eat anything with bread and something to wash it all down with. I enjoy cooking for myself.

Need: Bread—2 slices—whole wheat is best, mustard, onion, cheese your choice, vegetables, like green pepper, tomato, yellow or green beans, asparagus, eggplant, or the like, and alfalfa sprouts, plus a flat pan, and an oven heated to about 300 degrees. I shouldn't forget a camera on your shoulder for looks.

To make it, you:

1)	Place the bread on the flat pan, and mustard on one or both pieces.

2)	Place vegetables on both halves—lots of them—then place the sprouts on top of that.

3)	Grate the cheese (slices will do too), and sprinkle lots of it on both pieces of bread.

4)	Now add the onion slices to the top of the pile, some on each half.

5)	Place all of this in your hot oven. Be careful here you don't let your camera slip off your shoulder.

6)	When done, 5–10 minutes, place both halves together!

28	Bill Arnold, Breakfast Note,
	1979

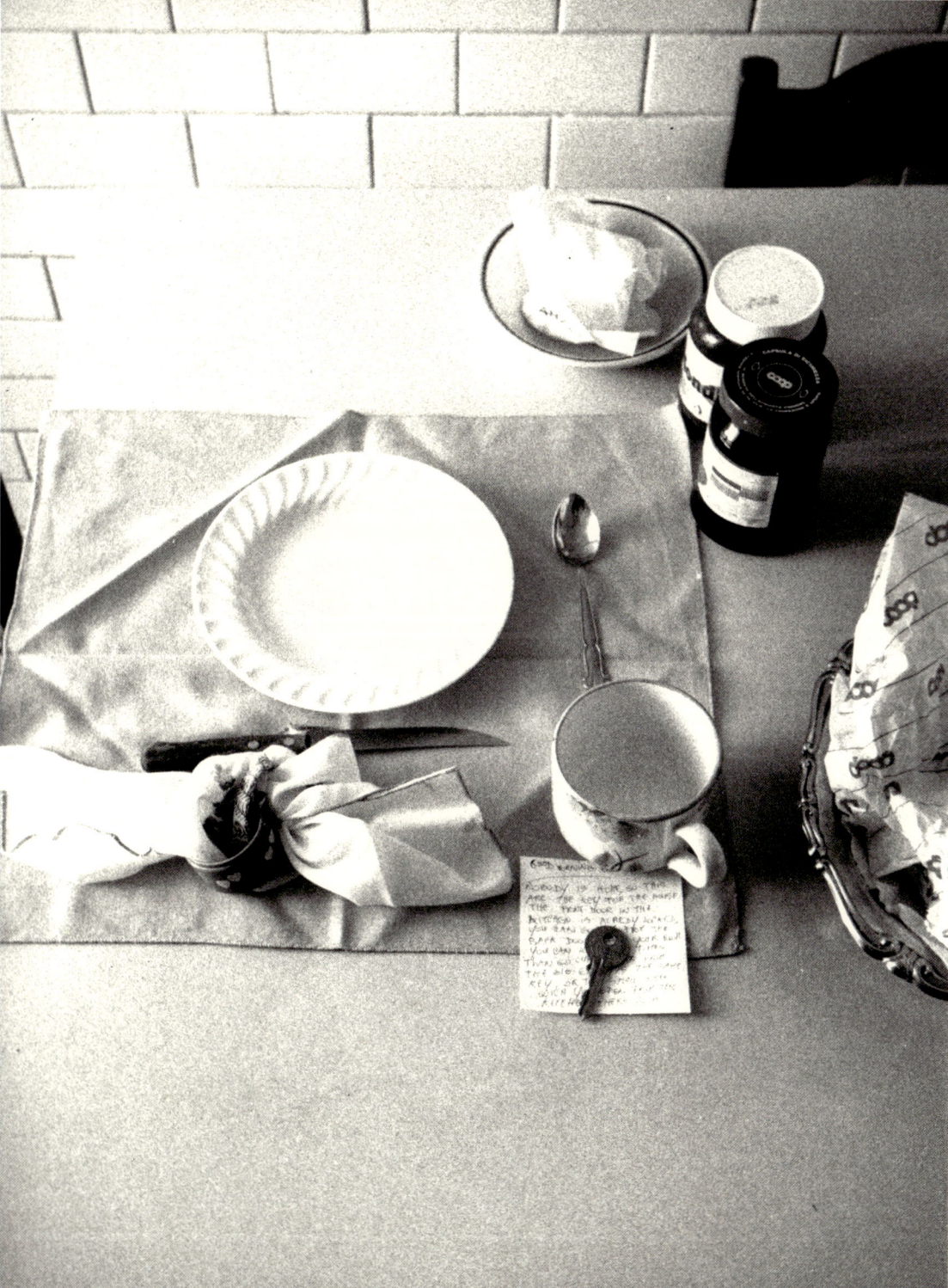

Thomas and Laurie Barrow: B & L's Burritos

Bean Filling
    2 tablespoons bacon fat
    2 strips bacon (optional)
    ¾ pound pinto beans

Beef Filling
    1 pound ground beef
    Ground black pepper

Salsa
    1 large yellow onion, chopped
    2 cloves garlic, minced
    2 medium tomatoes, peeled and chopped
    6 to 8 fresh, roasted, peeled, and chopped green chilies or
        1 (4-ounce) can chopped green chilies
    2 or 3 yellow wax chilies, finely chopped (HOT), or you may
        use 2 or 3 jalapeño chilies, finely chopped (very HOT),
        or you may use Tabasco to taste if no chilies are available
        (a last resort since it alters the flavor considerably)
    2 beef bouillon cubes dissolved in 2 cups boiling water

Burritos
    ½ pound grated longhorn style (Colby) cheese
    4 large (10- to 12-inch) flour tortillas
    Chopped yellow onion (optional)

1)   Cook beans for 3 or more hours in 5–6 cups water (more
    if needed) seasoned with 2 tablespoons bacon fat; additional
    flavor may be obtained by adding 2 strips of bacon the last
    half hour of cooking.

30   Thomas F. Barrow, Untitled,
    1973; from the portfolio Trivia 2

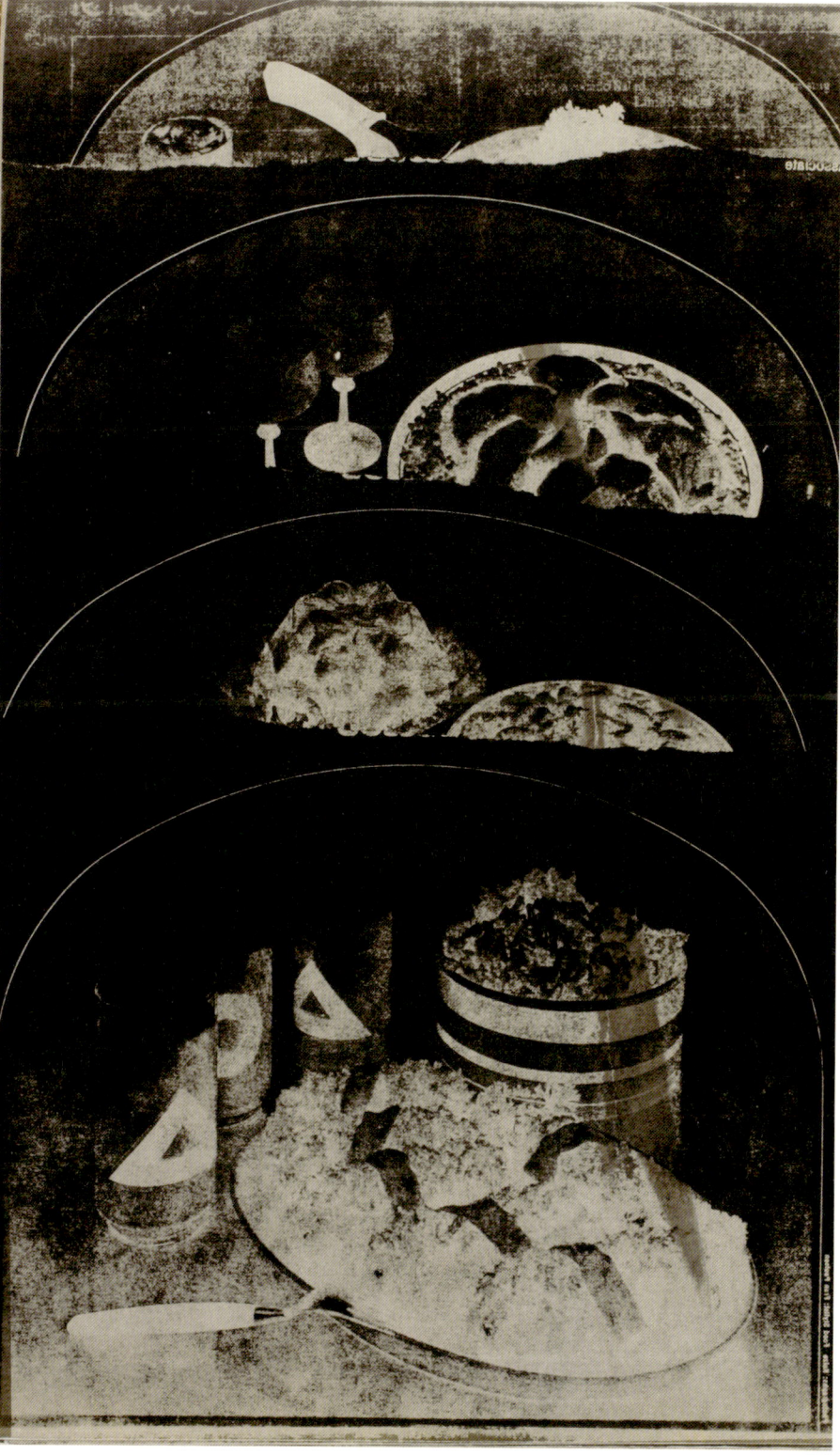

2) Make salsa. Sauté onions and garlic in saucepan until transparent; add tomatoes, green chilies, yellow wax chilies, and beef bouillon cubes dissolved in water, and simmer for 1 hour.

3) When the beans and salsa are ready, sauté the ground beef in an iron skillet until browned, adding ground black pepper to taste, drain.

To assemble burritos:

For each serving, place 1 flour tortilla on an ovenproof plate. Across the center place beef, beans, cheese, and salsa. Roll "stuffed" tortilla into a tube. Place a side of beans on each plate. Spread tortilla and beans with additional salsa and cheese. Place in 350-degree oven until cheese begins to melt; serve at once. Top with chopped yellow onion, if desired.

Serves 4.

Jerry Burchard's Caviar "Fish" Appetizer

"Fish"

1 brick cream cheese
1 (15-ounce) jar Romanoff Lumpfish Caviar (about $6.00 or $7.00)

Marination Sauce

1 pomegranate (juice and a small wedge for "fish's" mouth)
1 bundle fresh basil sprigs, crushed

½ pound or a couple cans button mushrooms
1 jar pimentos or 1 red bell pepper
1 lime

Toast or crackers

1) Shape 1 large brick of cream cheese into a fish on a platter
    or tray (about ⅓ size of dish).

2) Heap with iced caviar.

3) Put a wedge of pomegranate in the fish's mouth, and
    suggest fins and gill with strips of pimento or red
    bell pepper.

4) Garnish the surrounding rim with sprigs of basil and raw
    or canned button mushrooms.

5) Refrigerate until just before serving, then pour
    on marination sauce (see below), and furnish with heaps
    of toast or crackers. Add 2 or 3 butter knives or spreaders.

Marination sauce:
    Take 1 pomegranate, cut a small wedge for garnish
    (see above), and squeeze the rest for juice into a small bowl.
    Squeeze the juice from 1 lime. Mix the lime juice and
    pomegranate juice together, and pour juice mixture over
    a bowl of crushed basil sprigs. Let sit for a few minutes
    so that flavors come together. Strain out basil sprigs, and
    pour marination sauce over "fish" just before serving.

Serves dozens.

33 Jerry Burchard, Caviar,
    1978

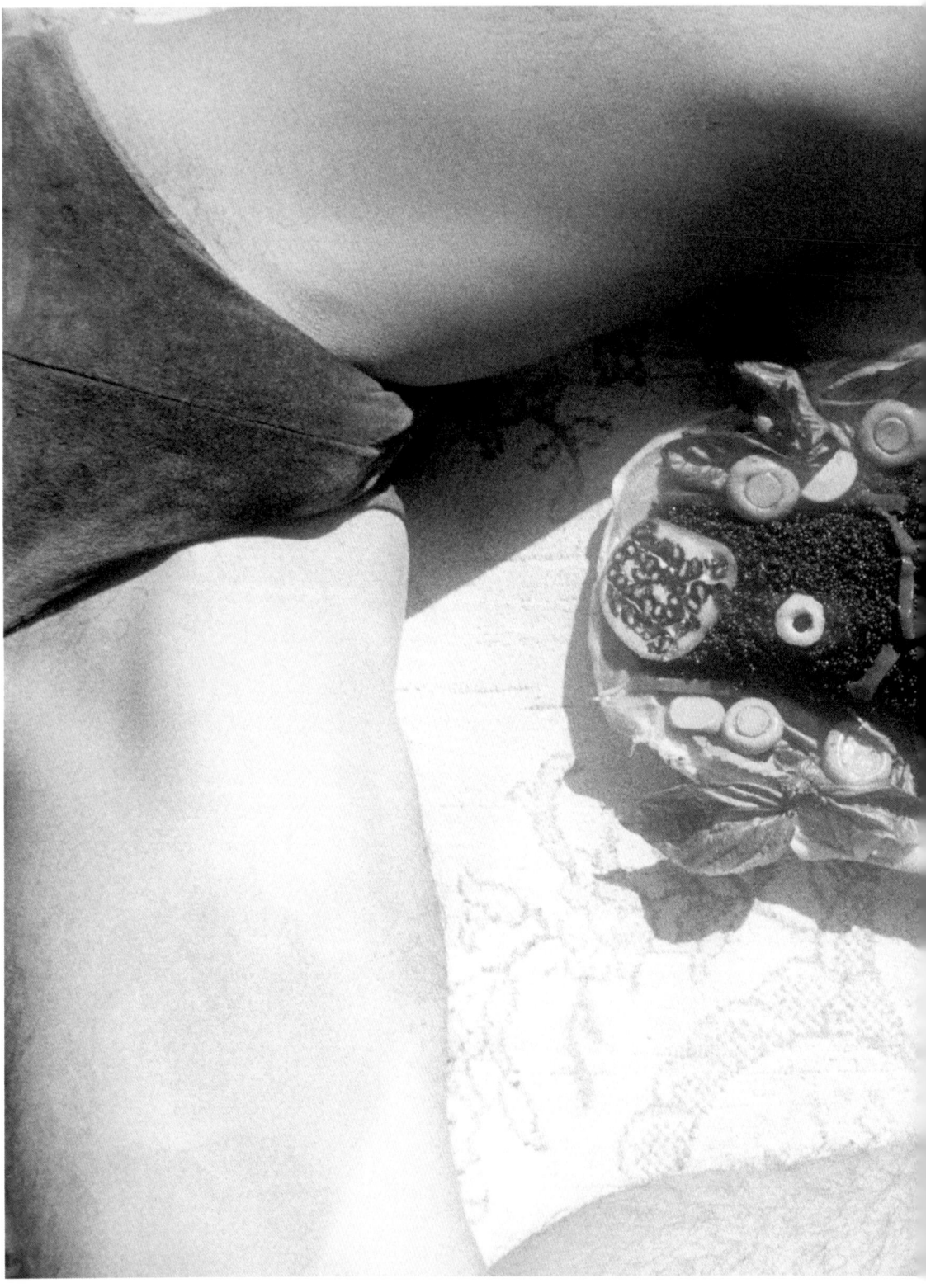

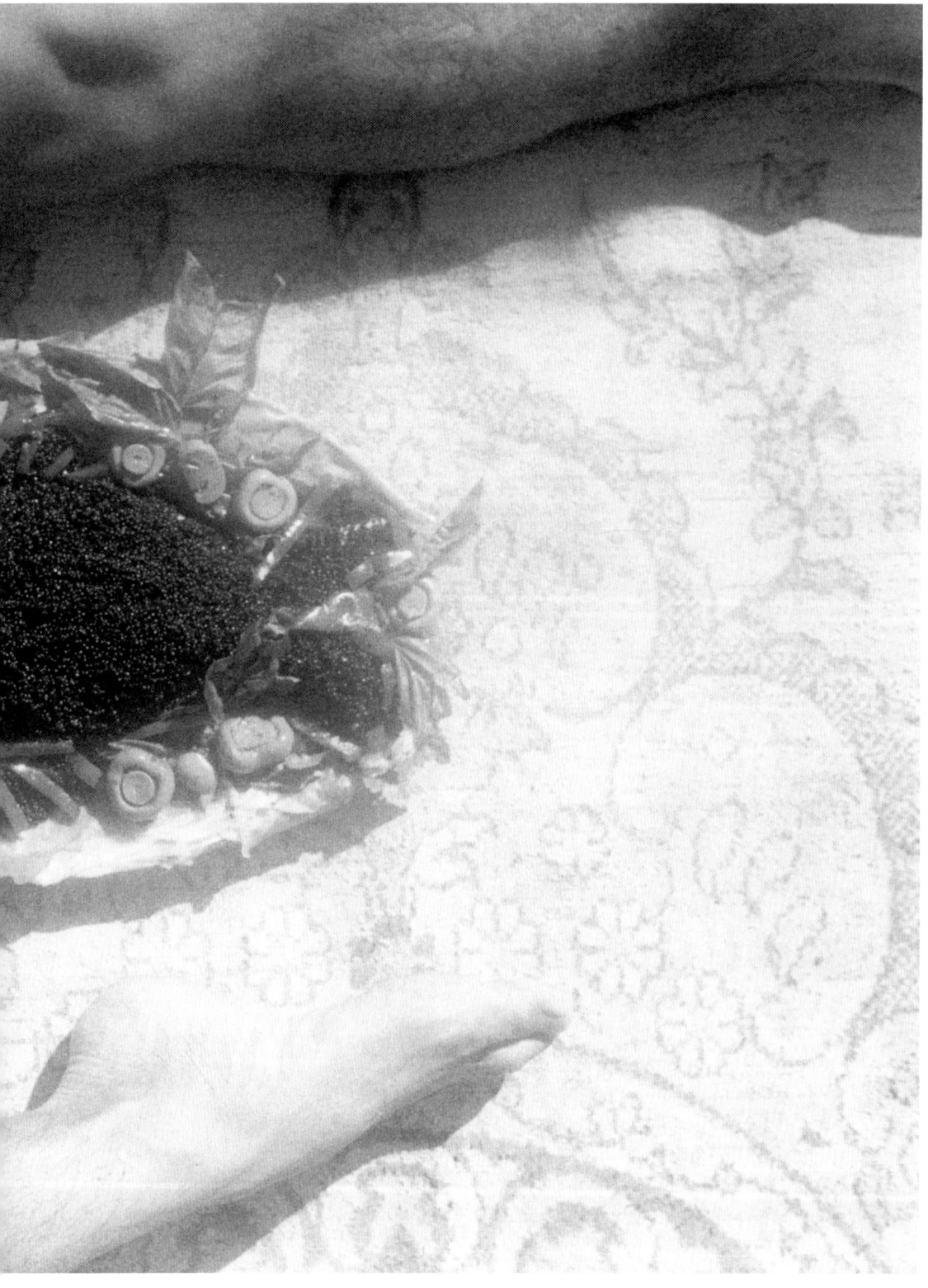

Neal Slavin: Nylen's Frankfurters in Full Dress

My most delightful and favorite "tidbit gastronomique" is called the "Nylen Full-Dress Frank." It's named after a professional colleague, Judy Nylen, who not by chance is also its creator . . .

The frankfurter need not be left naked! It can be formalized, decked out, and ethnicized for a sumptuous midnight snack or fun party fare. Condiments, garnishes, and accents can take on any theme. Those described below are "regional costumes" to be grouped buffet style for a party so guests can create their own masterpieces.

Basics: For a party of 24
    48 frankfurters
    48 buns

Bring 6 quarts of water to a boil in one or more large pots. Remove pots from heat, and put in frankfurters. Cover and let stand 7 minutes. Frankfurters can be served right from the pot, or kept warm on a hot tray set on low. They will last several hours in warm water.

Buns can be warmed in an electric bun warmer or an improvised version created by placing a basket in an electric frying pan or wok, wrapping buns in a large napkin, and covering.

DRESSINGS:

New Yorker
    2 cups sauerkraut
Heat sauerkraut through and keep warm on hot tray;
smother frankfurter.

German
    1 cup applesauce
    1 cup crab apples, sliced
Spoon applesauce over frankfurter, and garnish with
crab apples.

Californian
    1 pint cherry tomatoes, sliced
    1 head curly Spanish lettuce
    ½ cup Thousand Island dressing
Place lettuce under frankfurter which has been sliced
lengthwise; stuff with tomato slices down the center and top
with dressing.

Southern
    2 cups frozen macaroni and cheese, baked according
        to package
    ½ pound bacon, cut in half and fried lightly crisp
    1 cup cheddar cheese
Spoon macaroni onto bun, put in frankfurter, cover with a little
more macaroni, top with bacon and grated cheese, and melt in
toaster oven.

37   Neal Slavin, Frankfurters in Full Dress,
     1978

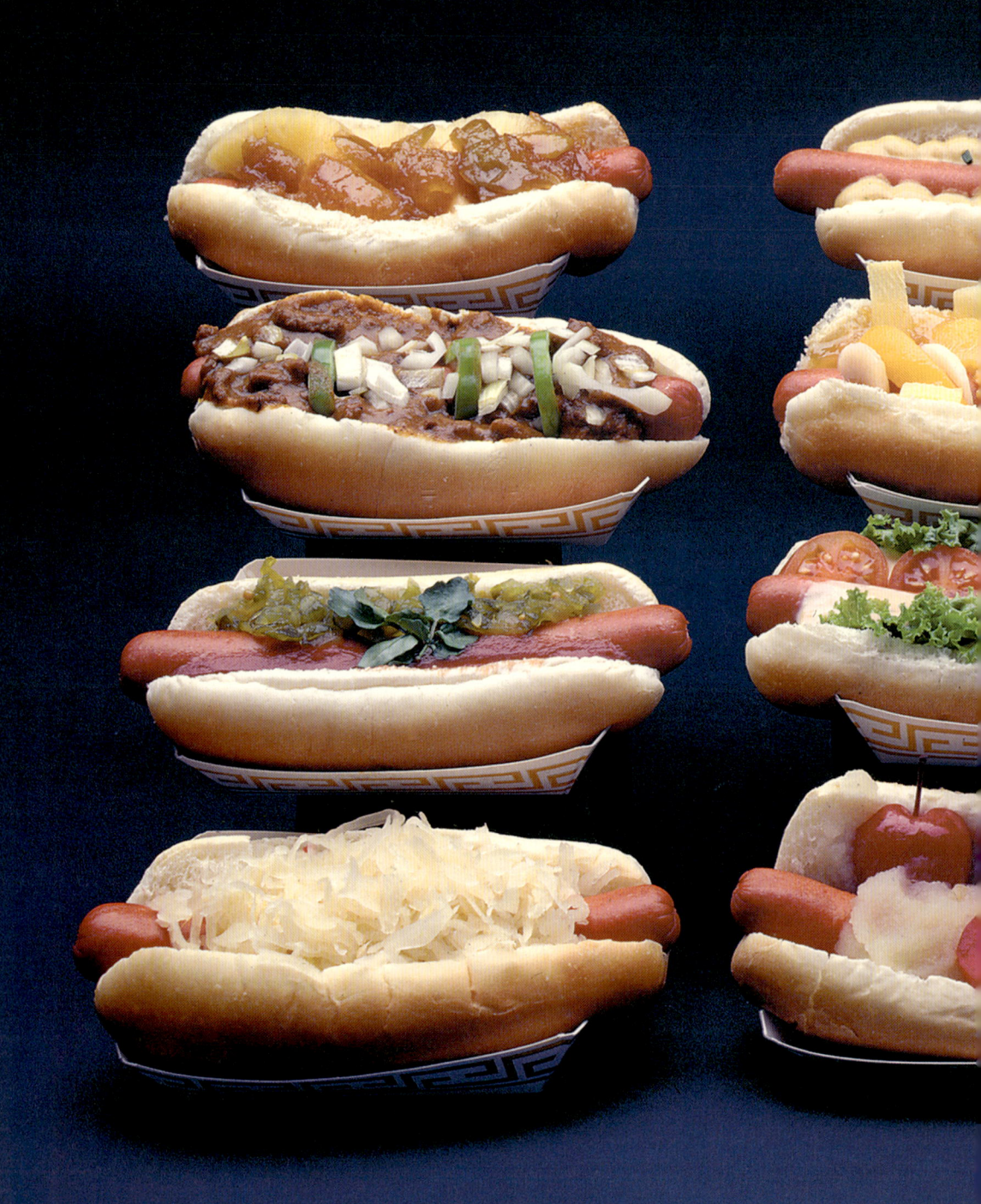

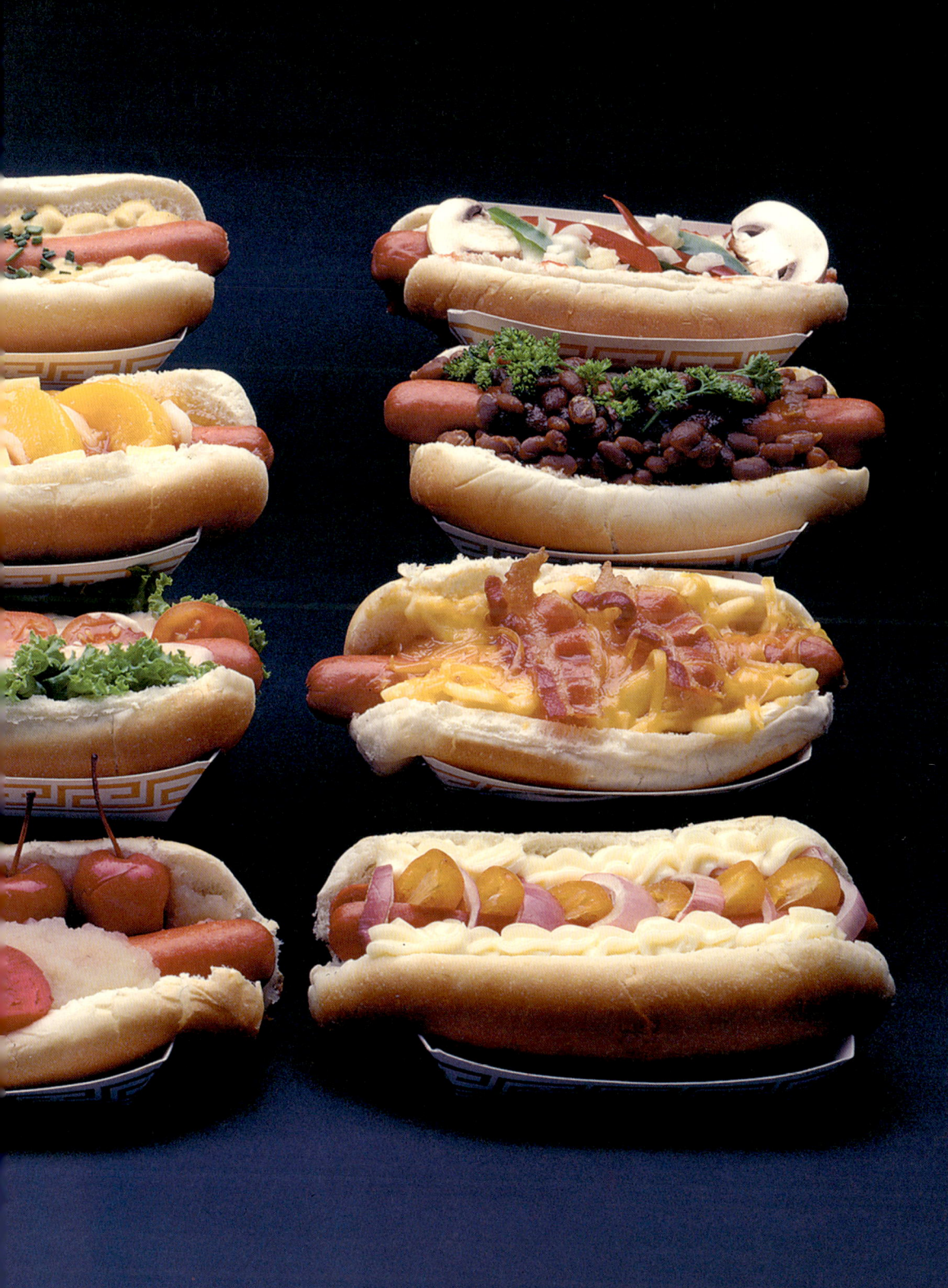

Mexican
      4 frying peppers, in rings
      2 cups chili, without beans
      1 cup onion, finely chopped
Heat chili through, and keep warm on hot tray. String peppers,
3 or 4, onto frankfurter, and top with chili and onions.

Chinese
      ½ cup water chestnuts, sliced
      1 cup canned sliced peaches
      ½ cup bamboo shoots, sliced
      ½ cup sweet and sour sauce
Cut frankfurter in short, diagonal slits, and stuff these with
water chestnuts. Top with peaches, bamboo shoots, and sauce.

Middle Eastern
      1 cup kumquats, peeled and quartered
      1 large red onion, sliced in rings
      ½ cup mayonnaise
Slice frankfurter lengthwise and stuff with 3 or 4 kumquat
quarters, alternating with red onion. Surround with mayonnaise.

Irish
      2 cups pickle relish—Emerald style
      1 small bunch watercress
Smother frankfurter in relish, and garnish with watercress
"clovers."

New Englander
      2 cups baked beans
      1 bunch curly parsley
Heat beans through, and keep warm on hot tray; spoon over
frankfurter, and garnish with parsley.

Polynesian

> 1 cup pineapple rings, halved
> ½ cantaloupe, cubed
> ½ cup Major Grey's Chutney (may substitute any
>   mango chutney)

Place pineapple rings over frankfurter, garnish with
cantaloupe, and top with chutney.

All-American

> 1 cup brown mustard (or any favorite)
> ¼ cup snipped chives

Smother frankfurter in traditional manner.

Italian

> 1 cup pizza sauce
> 1 cup grated mozzarella cheese
> 1 red bell pepper, in thin strips
> 1 green pepper, sliced in thin strips
> 12 fresh mushrooms, sliced

Keep pizza sauce warm on hot tray. Spoon over bun, put in
frankfurter, and top with grated cheese, pepper strips, and
mushrooms. Put frankfurter in toaster oven to melt cheese.

Paul Vanderbilt's Buffet Salads

I put on the buffet table two large, substantial meat and fish salads with a selection of cheese, crackers, and fruit. The salads don't have a fancy name, but they're easy to make, and my friends seem to come back for more.

For one salad, get "Smokey Links" sausages, about 4 per person, slit them lengthwise and grill them slowly, cut side up, under the broiler until well browned. Cut sausages into bite-size pieces. Slice cold cucumbers very thin in a big bowl, and combine with sausages, about 2 parts sausages to 3 parts cucumber. Add liberally: olive oil, fresh ground pepper, dill weed, tarragon, dry mustard, vinegar, and a little salt. Toss-mix well.

For the other salad, combine in a large bowl about equal parts of chopped raw yellow onions, canned oil-packed tuna fish, and sliced boiled potatoes. Use whole, small, red new potatoes, do not overcook, and leave the skins on. Add liberally: olive oil, fresh ground pepper, dill weed, sweet basil, chopped parsley, lemon juice, vinegar, and a little salt. Mix well, but gently, not to break up the potato slices. Should be quite moist.

This is all a bit sharp and sour; so compensate with at least some mild cheese and sweet fruits like fresh pineapple and large Anjou pears. My idea of crackers is Weston Foods Ltd. (Toronto) Biscotins de Blé Concassé (Stoned Wheat Thins).

42   Paul Vanderbilt, Interior of Bush's Cafe,
       1963

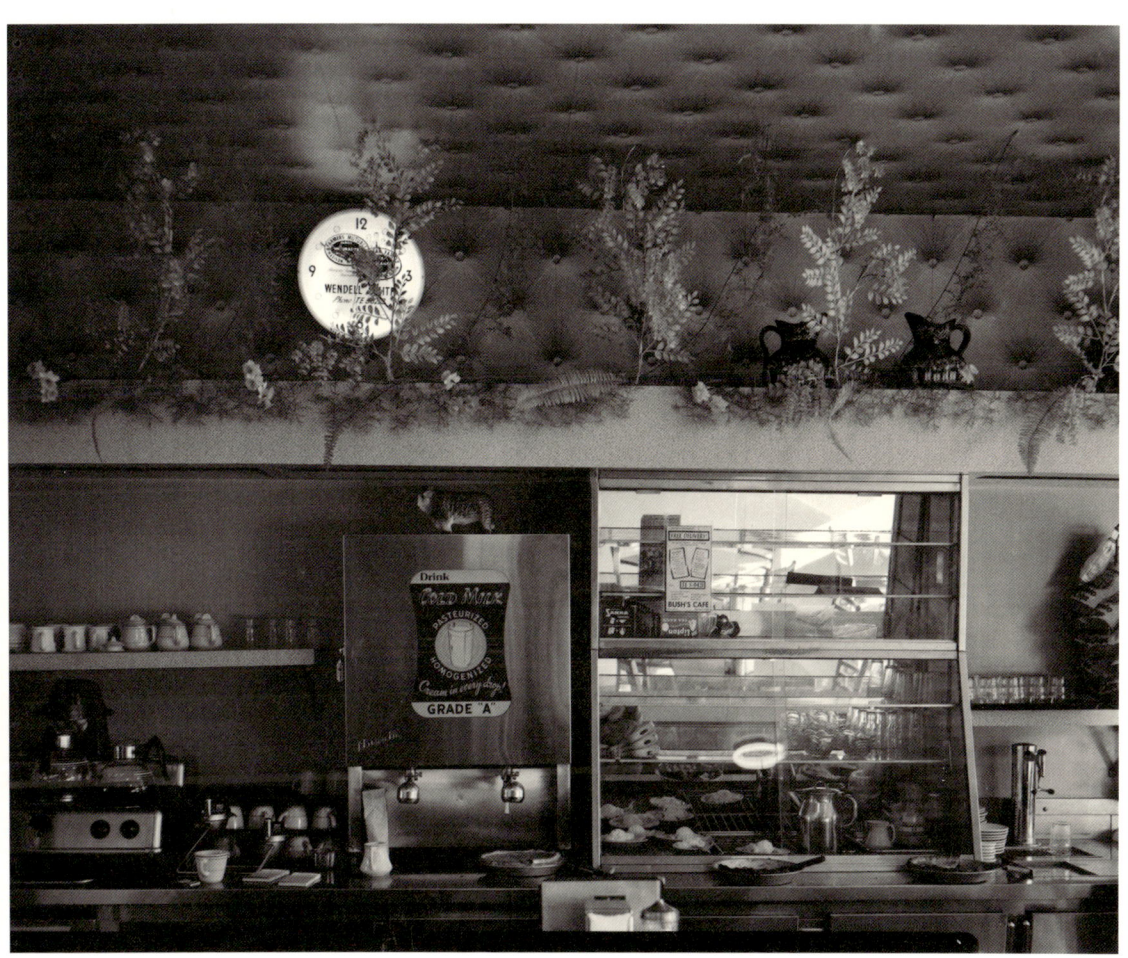

Soups

Lewis Baltz: Mary Ann Baltz's She-Crab Soup

1 tablespoon butter
1 tablespoon flour
1 quart milk
2 cups fresh crab meat
1 small onion, finely chopped
1 teaspoon Worcestershire sauce
2 teaspoons lemon juice
1 teaspoon mace
4 tablespoons dry sherry
Salt
Pepper
½ pint whipped cream
Chopped parsley

1)   Melt butter in double boiler. Add flour to make
     a smooth paste.

2)   Slowly add milk, stirring constantly. Warm this mixture
     for a few minutes.

3)   Add crab meat, onion, Worcestershire sauce, lemon juice,
     and mace.

4)   Cook slowly for ½ hour.

5)   Then salt and pepper to taste. Turn off heat, and let soup
      rest for 10 minutes.

6)   Then add sherry.

When serving, float whipped cream on soup, and sprinkle with
chopped parsley.

Note:
      Traditionally, this soup is made with both the meat and
      eggs of the crab, hence the name "she-crab" soup. In
      California it is not legal to sell crab eggs, so this recipe
      does not call for them.

47   Lewis Baltz, San Francisco,
      1973

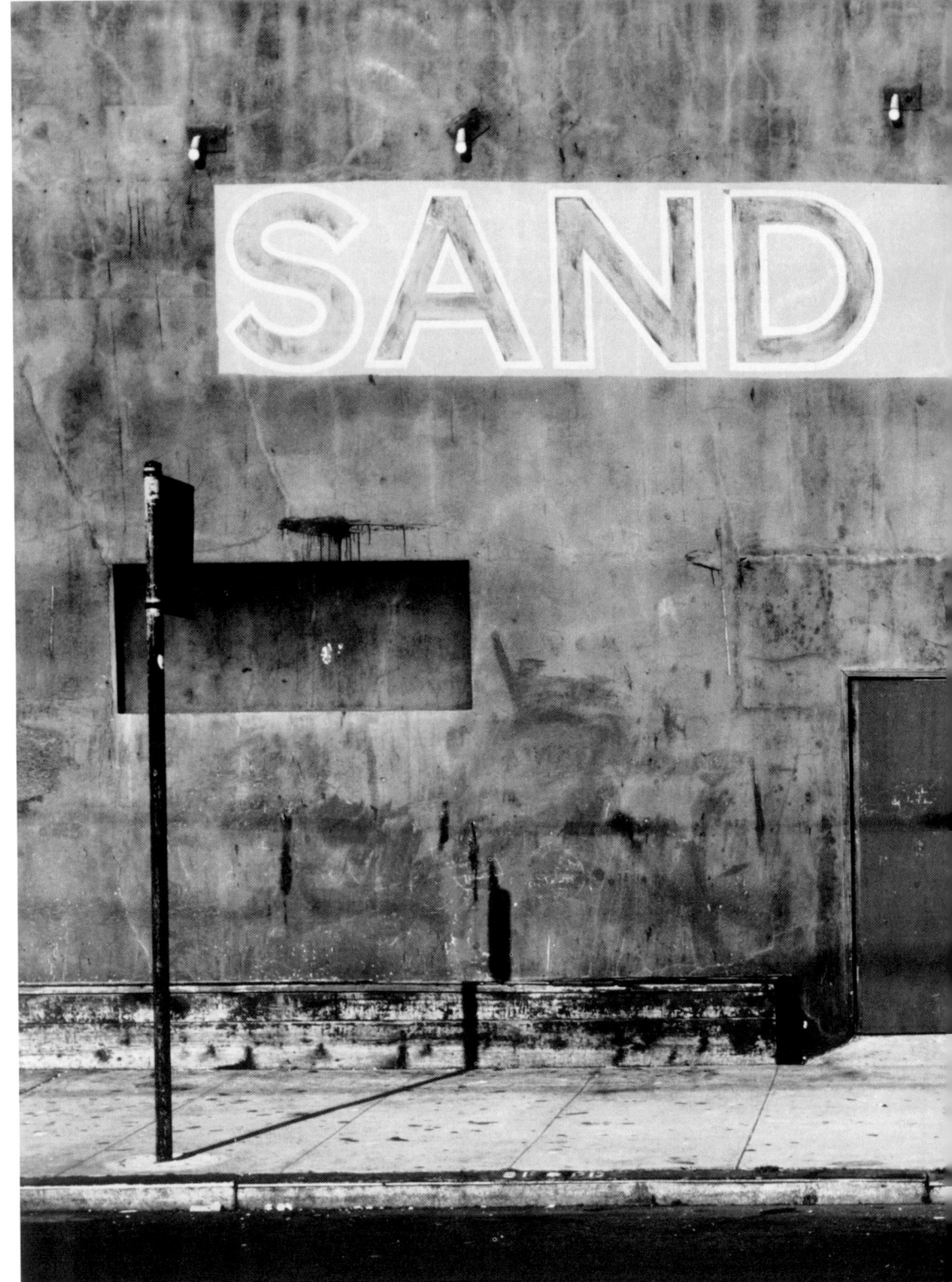

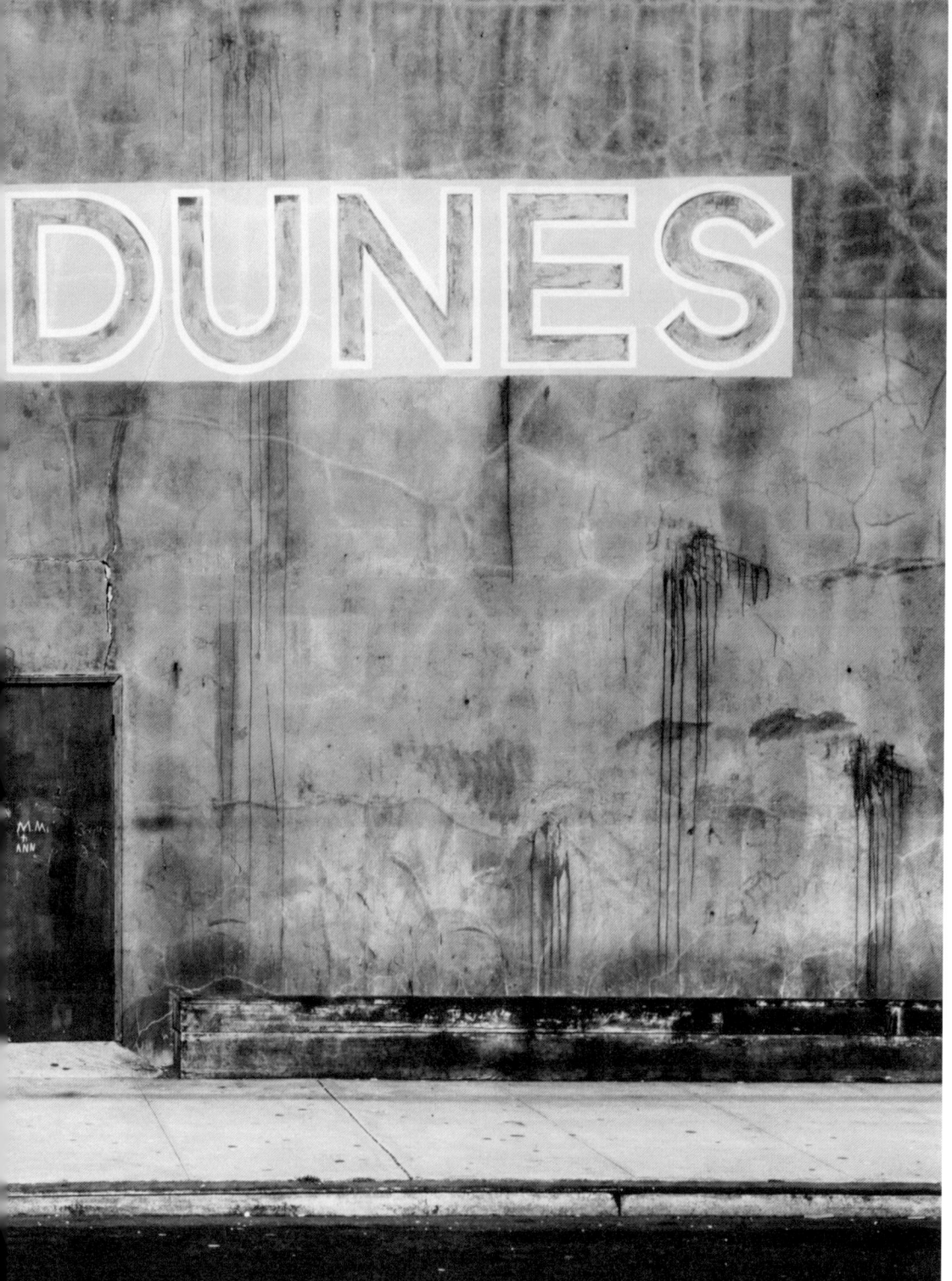

Linda Connor's
Pumpkin-Pomegranate Soup

2 tablespoons butter
1 onion, chopped
1 teaspoon curry powder (or to taste)
1 tablespoon flour
2 cans chicken stock
1 pound canned pumpkin
1 teaspoon brown sugar
⅛ teaspoon nutmeg
Salt
Pepper
Parsley
1 cup light cream
Pomegranate seeds (or raisins)

Sauté chopped onion in butter. Stir in curry powder and flour. Add chicken stock, pumpkin, brown sugar, nutmeg, salt, pepper, and parsley. Simmer 10 minutes or so; it should reach a boil. Remove from heat. Stir in cream. Serve immediately.

Serve with pomegranate seeds sprinkled over soup. Raisins can be used as a poor substitute.

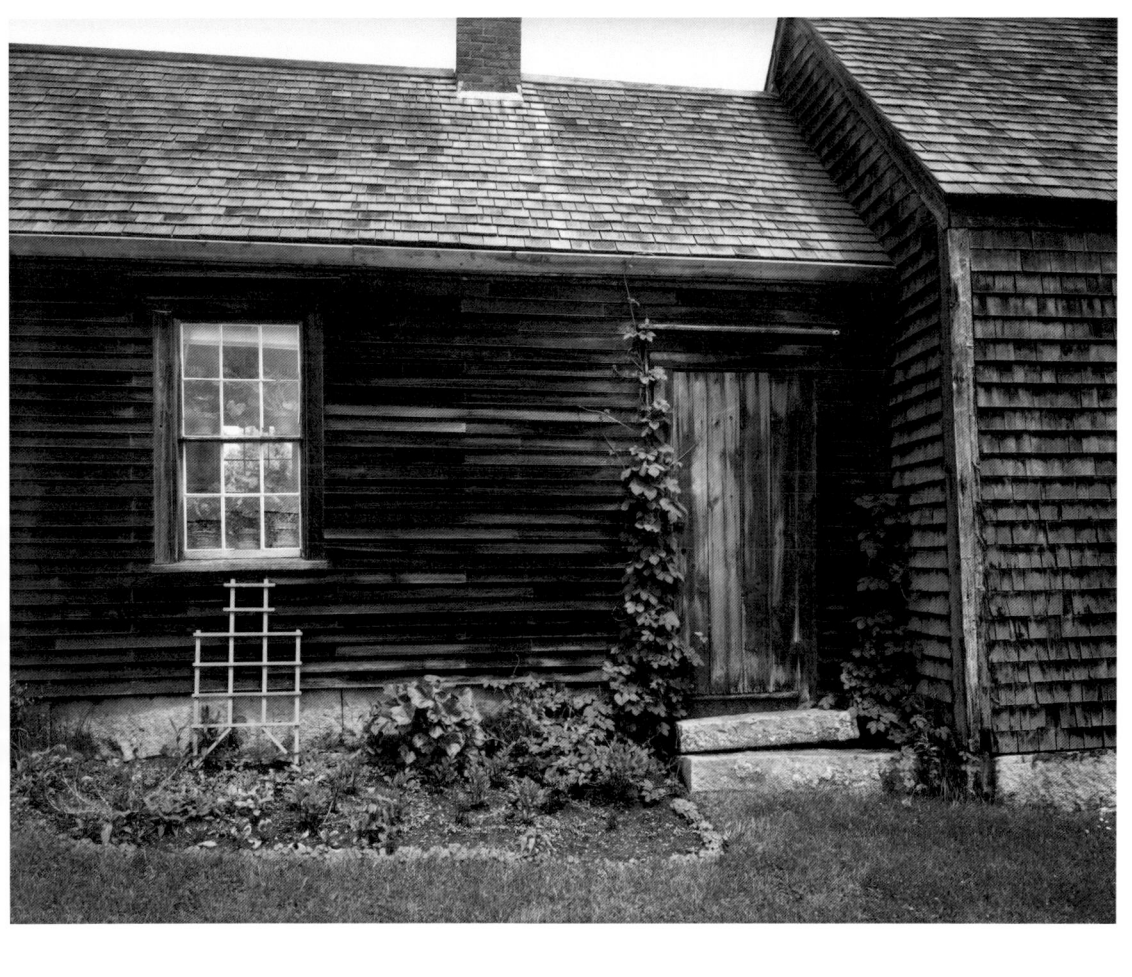

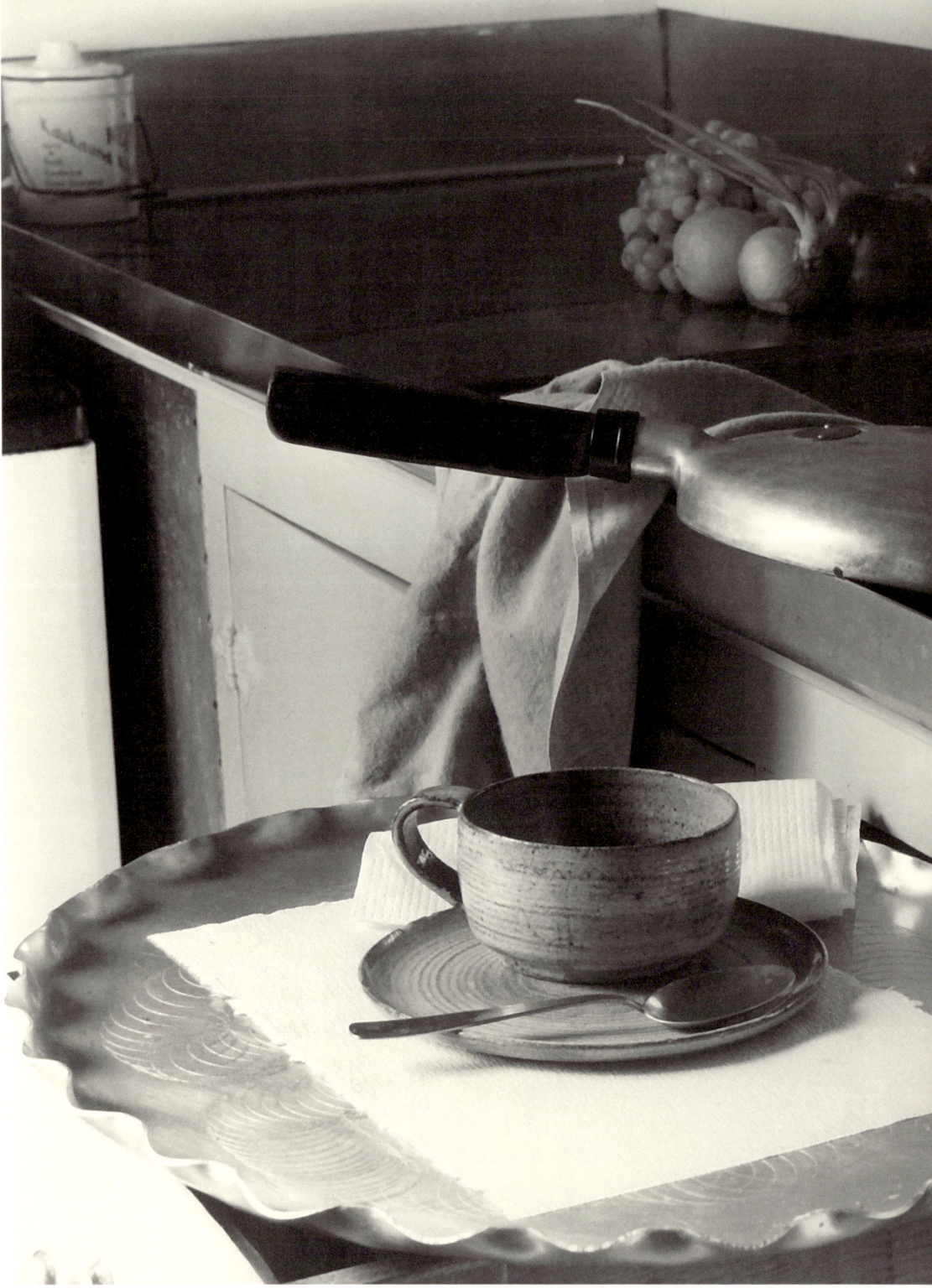

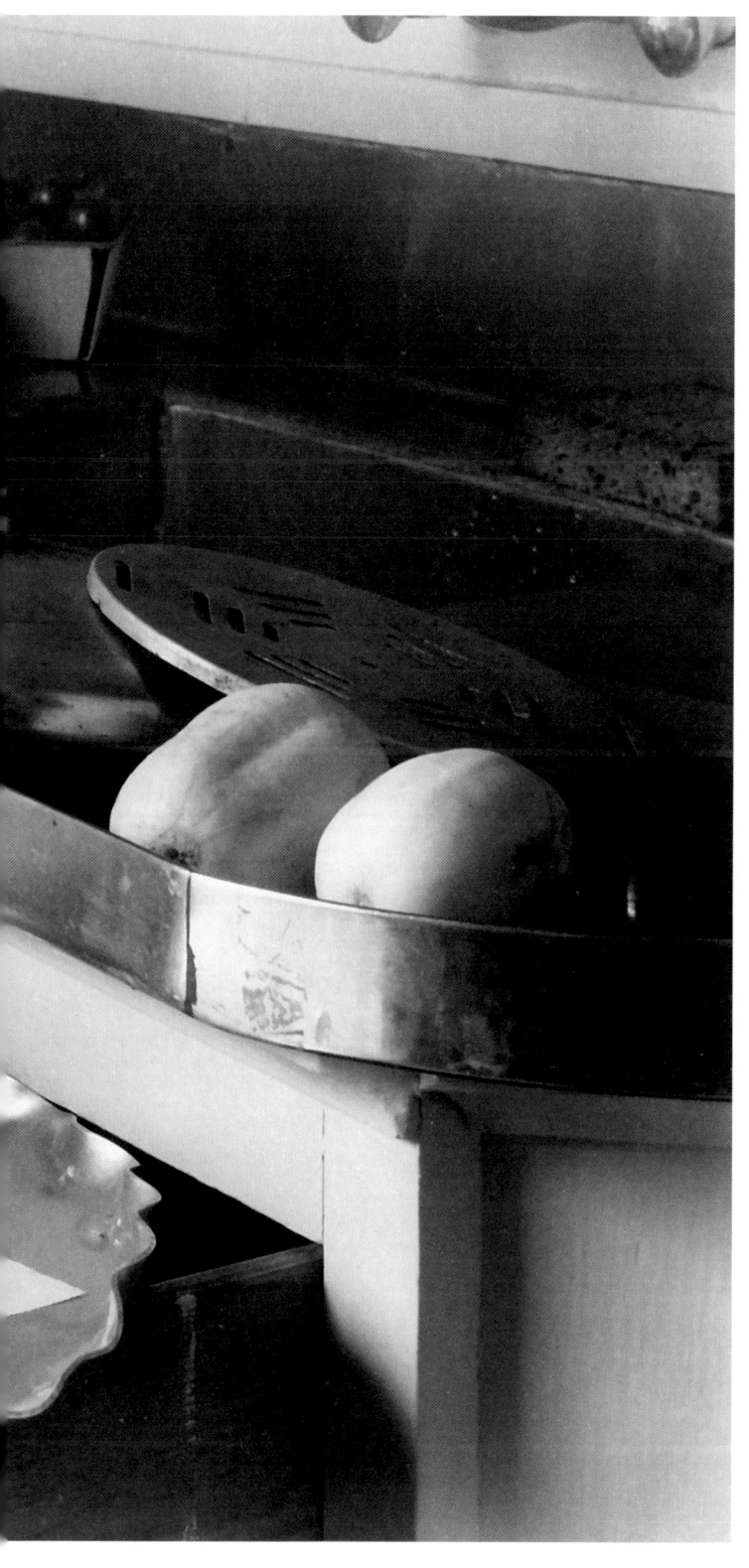

Imogen Cunningham's Borscht

For one thing I do not consider Alice B. Toklas a GREAT cook.
Very likely her cooking contributed to the death of Gertrude
and herself. Besides her beef stew cooked in burgundy, I can
think only of her beautiful soups beginning with gazpacho from
everywhere. I do not know how to put it, but exotic eatery is
very interesting to me. I think we are all TOO addicted to salt
and that we can get enough in vegetables that offer it. We do
not know the flavor of anything because we doctor it too much.
While I am on soups, I should tell you what I do for borscht.
I make a good soup of beef and meat and bones; put some fresh
beets in, and when I am ready to serve it, I make it half mine
and half Manischewitz (commercial bottle of borscht). I prefer
it cold with sour cream.

Burt Glinn's Borscht
"À la My Grandmother with an Assist
from Eliot Elisofon"

1½ pounds shinbone of beef, cut into 2-inch-thick pieces
with marrow inside them. (If you can't get 1½ pounds
of shinbone from the butcher, ask him to augment the
available shinbone with other pieces of soup bone.)
3 pounds beef brisket, cut into 1-inch cubes
1 head cabbage, shredded
1 large (35-ounce) can peeled Italian tomatoes, preferably
with basil leaf

54   Imogen Cunningham, My Kitchen Sink,
1947

2 large onions, chopped
6 cloves garlic, minced
1 bay leaf
1 teaspoon paprika
1 teaspoon salt
Fresh ground pepper
3 tablespoons lemon juice
3 tablespoons sugar
18 small new potatoes, peeled
Fresh dill
Sour cream

Equipment
Large kettle or soup pot
Tureen

Place all the pieces of bone and cubed brisket of beef into the kettle or pot. Top with the entire head of shredded cabbage. Pour in the canned tomatoes. Add chopped onions, minced garlic, bay leaf, paprika, and add salt and ground pepper to taste. Add lemon juice and sugar. Add enough cold water to completely cover meat. (Cabbage will float to top.) Cover and simmer for at least 3 hours.

While the borscht is simmering, skim the accumulated fat off the top. The borscht is better on the second day than the first and even better on the third day. If you have the luxury of making it over a 2-day period, the best method is to simmer it for 3–4 hours on the first day, then let it cool thoroughly. If you have room in the fridge you might even place it in the icebox. After it has cooled down and the fat has coagulated on the top, it is much easier to separate.

(Somehow the borscht always tastes better if you take this extra
time to cool and skim off the fat.)

To serve, bring borscht back to a slow boil and simmer again.
Thirty minutes before serving, add the potatoes so that they can
be cooked thoroughly by serving time. When the potatoes
are done, the borscht is ready to be prepared for serving. Remove
all the bones and any gristle from the pot with a slotted spoon.
Separate all the pieces of meat onto one platter and the cooked
potatoes onto another platter. Place hot borscht into tureen
you've warmed. Ladle the stock into deep soup bowls. Add
appropriate amount of meat and potatoes to each serving. Top
with sour cream, and sprinkle with fresh dill.

Note:
>This is a flexible recipe, and your taste should be your
>guide. I find that the most important thing is the balance
>between the lemon juice and the sugar to give it that
>Slavic sweet/sour taste. Some people like to add beets
>to the kettle or pot at the very beginning, simmering
>them throughout the entire process and removing them
>just before serving when bones are removed, but my
>grandmother never used beets.

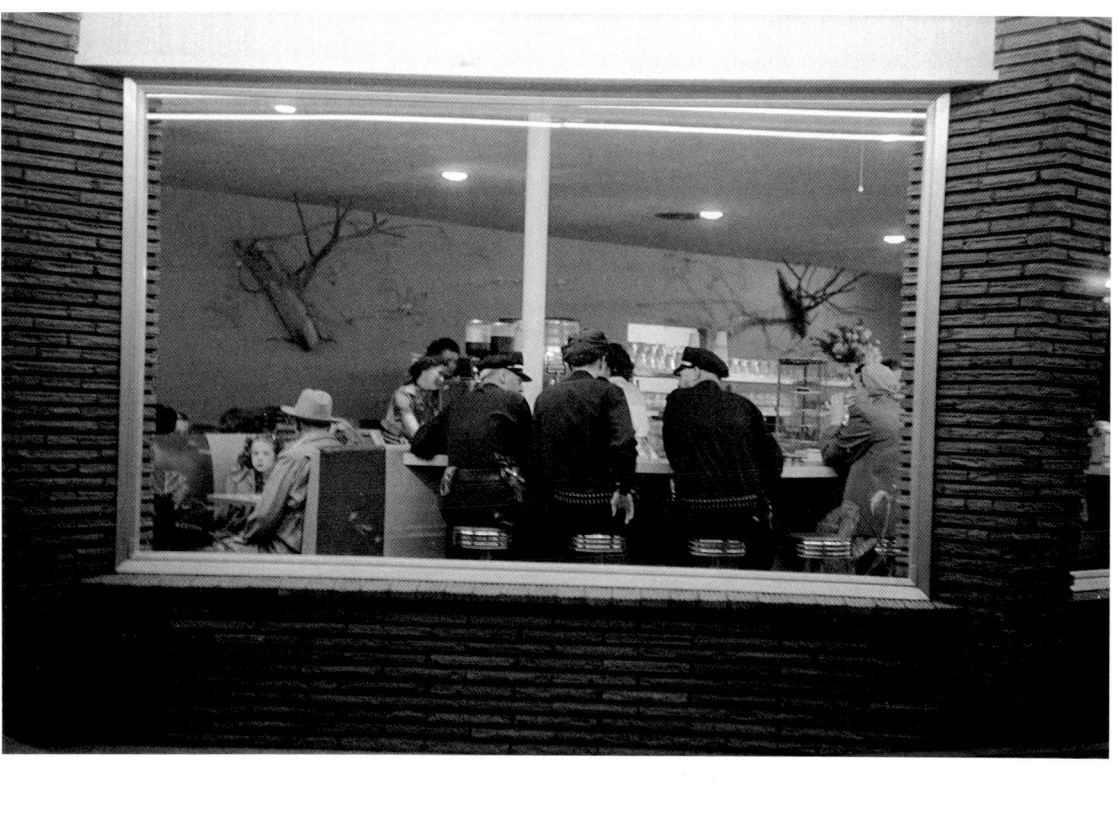

Bea Nettles's Nettles Soup

Some students at a workshop in Sun Valley, Idaho, invited me to their teepee to sample nettles soup in the summer of '75. It is simple and delicious . . . if you're lucky enough to live in an area where nettles grow.

1)   Pick a quantity of tender nettle leaves. Wear rubber gloves to avoid being stung.

2)   Place the washed nettle leaves in boiling water for about 30 seconds. Pour this water off . . . this takes the sting out of the leaves.

3)   Put the nettle leaves in a chicken broth, and simmer about 1 minute.

4)   Add a carton of cream, some salt and pepper, and enjoy.

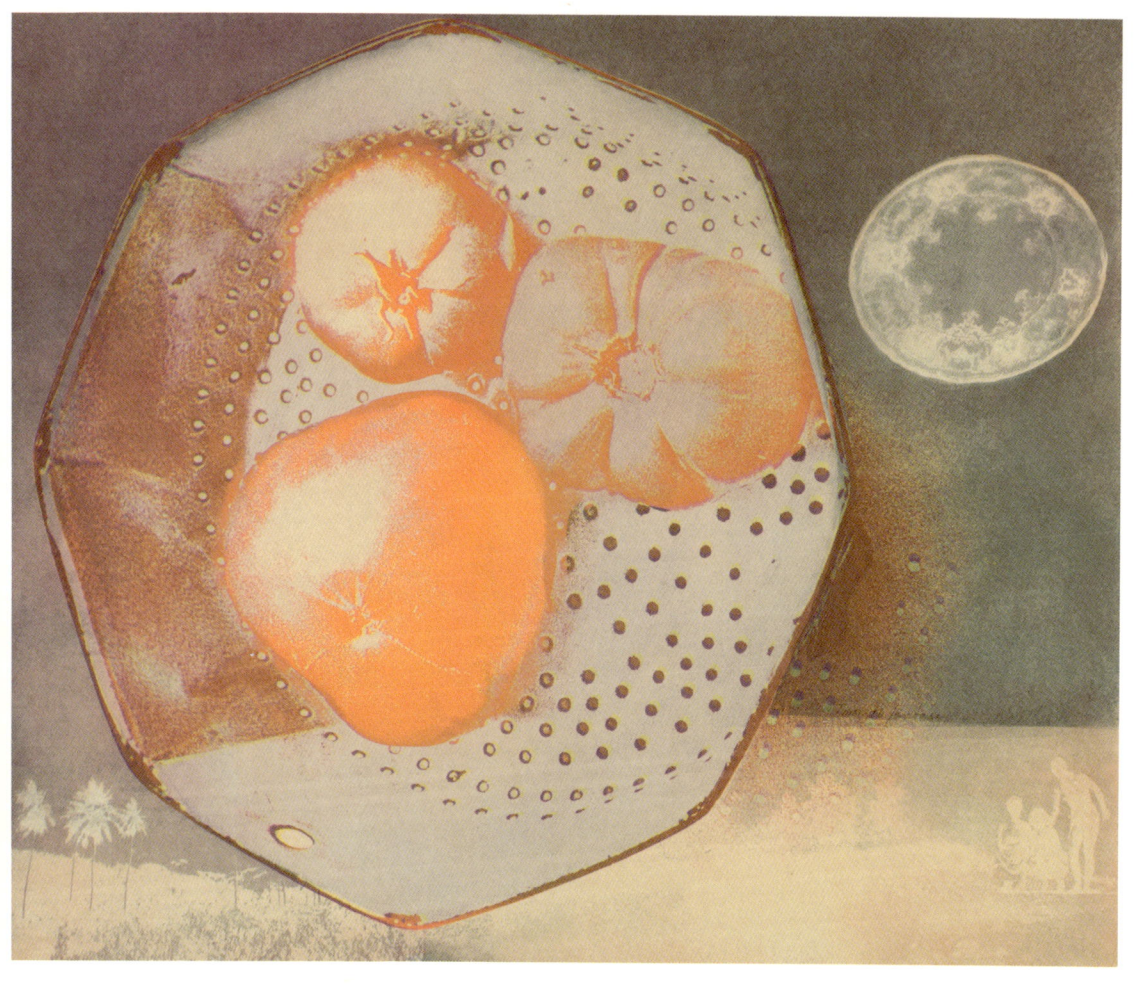

Main Dishes

Richard Avedon's The Royal Pot Roast

When we want GOOD FOOD, we call Anna Avedon, mother of the
photographer, for her famous recipe:

> 20 onions, chopped
> 7 pounds first-cut brisket
> 2 bay leaves
> 2 (16-ounce) cans whole tomatoes
> 2 (8-ounce) cans Del Monte tomato sauce (if tomato sauce is not
>   sharp enough, add tomato juice, salt, and pepper to taste)
> Sweet and sour red cabbage (from a jar)
> Caraway seeds
> Applesauce (optional)
> Orange rind, grated (optional)
> Rye bread, butter

1) Brown the onions, sear the meat, add the bay leaves, salt, and
   pepper. Cook in heavy iron pot or Dutch oven, covered, at 325
   degrees with small amount of water in bottom, for 3 hours.

2) Take the meat out, slice it, skim off fat, then put it back in
   the pot. Add Del Monte tomato sauce and whole tomatoes.
   Cook 30 minutes longer or until tender.

3) Serve with Greenwood sweet and sour red cabbage from a jar,
   and sprinkle caraway seeds on top. Also Seneca applesauce
   with a little grated orange rind stirred in goes nicely. This
   meal must be served with fresh rye bread and real butter.
   Tastes even better the next day reheated.

Serves 12.

62   Richard Avedon, Elise Daniels, Bracelet by Balmain,
Le Pré Catelan, Paris, 1948

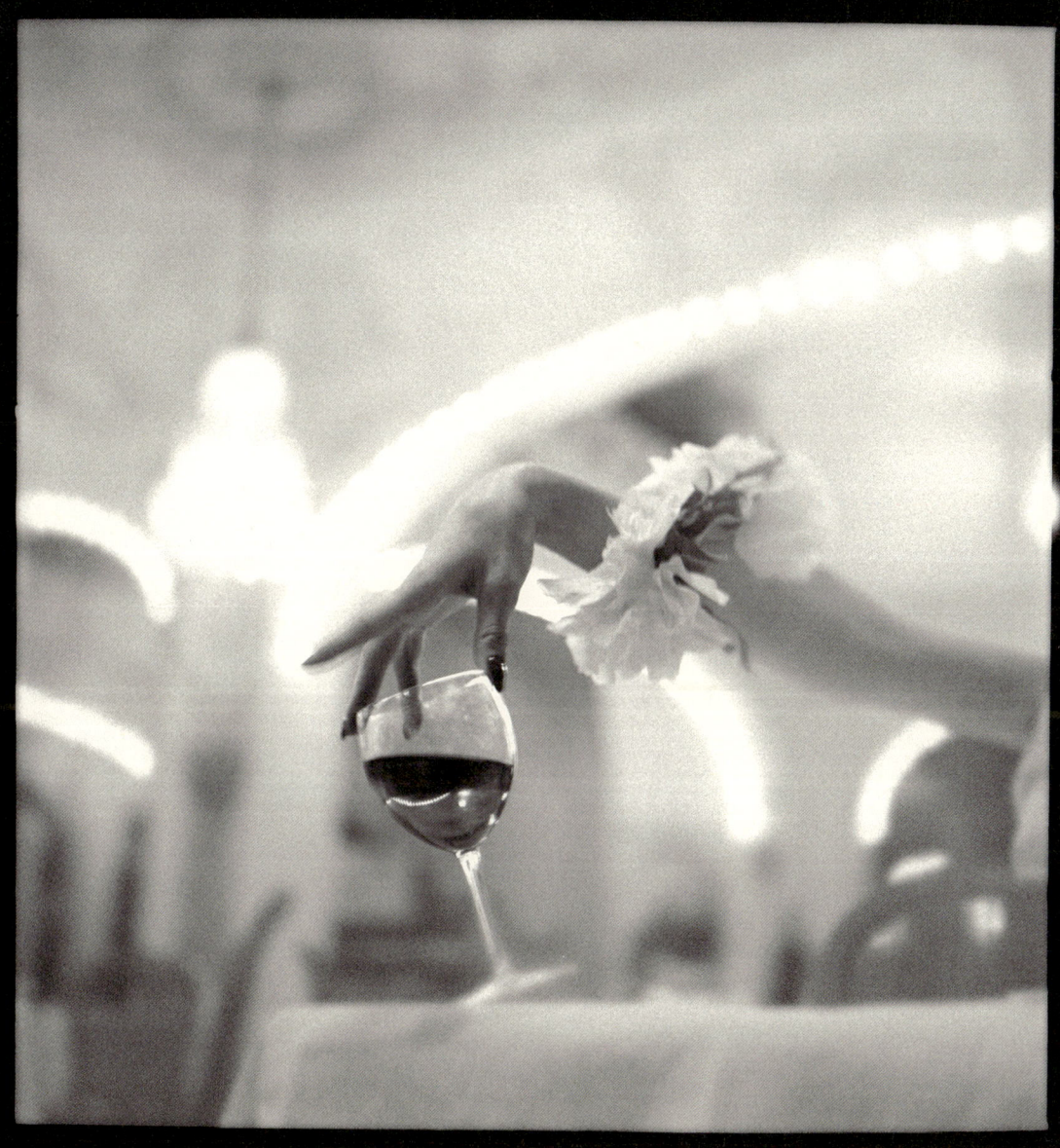

Wynn Bullock's Italian Spaghetti Sauce

Old family recipe given to my wife, Edna, many years ago
by an Italian friend.

In Dutch oven, brown well:

> 1½ pounds ground beef
>
> ¼ green pepper, chopped
>
> 2 medium onions, chopped
>
> 3 toes garlic
>
> ½ cup parsley, chopped or use scant tablespoon dry parsley
>
> 1 tablespoon Worcestershire sauce
>
> 1 teaspoon paprika
>
> ½ to ¾ teaspoon salt
>
> ½ teaspoon black pepper
>
> 1 tablespoon Italian herbs

Add:

> 2 (8-ounce) cans tomato sauce
>
> 2 (6-ounce) cans tomato paste plus 2 cans water
>
> 1 (4-ounce) can mushrooms or fresh mushrooms
>
> 2 tablespoons grated Parmesan cheese

Stir well. Cover and cook 1½ hours or until good and thick.
Serve over spaghetti cooked al dente.

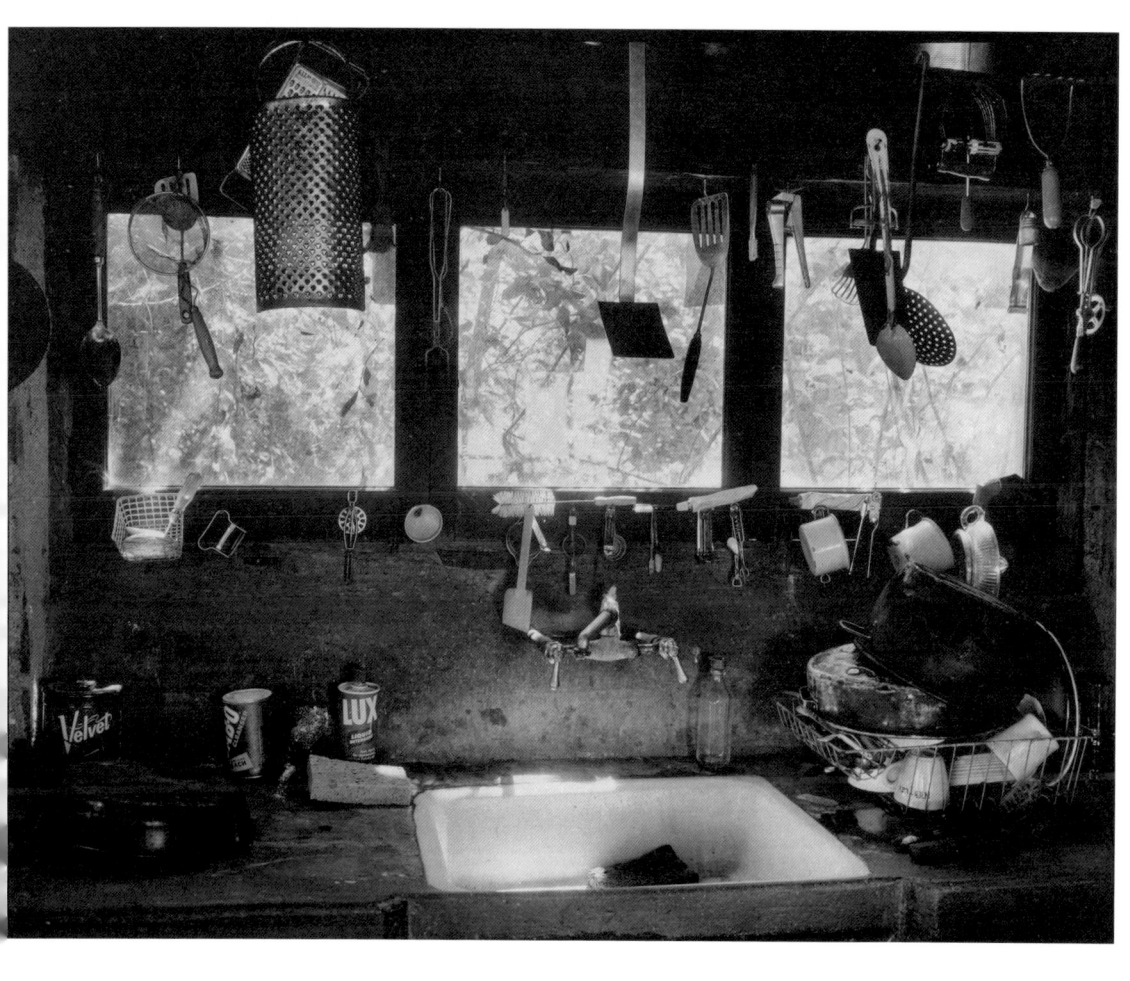

John Pfahl's Hamburgers au Slivovitz

I have been addicted to Slivovitz (the marvelous Yugoslavian
plum brandy) since I first encountered it while climbing
in the Austrian Alps seventeen years ago. There is always some
around the house, and I was delighted with the result when
I used it in place of regular brandy in this standard recipe for
Hamburgers au Poivre.

1½ pounds ground chuck
Salt to taste
2 tablespoons freshly ground or crushed peppercorns
2 tablespoons butter (divided)
1 tablespoon chopped green onions
¼ cup dry white wine
¼ cup bouillon
Juice from ½ lemon
1 tablespoon Slivovitz brandy
2 tablespoons chopped parsley

1) Form 4 patties with the ground chuck, and sprinkle with
   salt. Sprinkle all over with ground peppercorns, and press
   peppercorns into meat.

2) Heat a heavy iron skillet. When quite hot, add the meat
   patties, and cook about 5 minutes on one side.

3) Turn the patties over with a spatula and cook about
   5 minutes longer (10 minutes, if you want them well done).

66 John Pfahl, Hamburgers au Slivovitz,
    1978

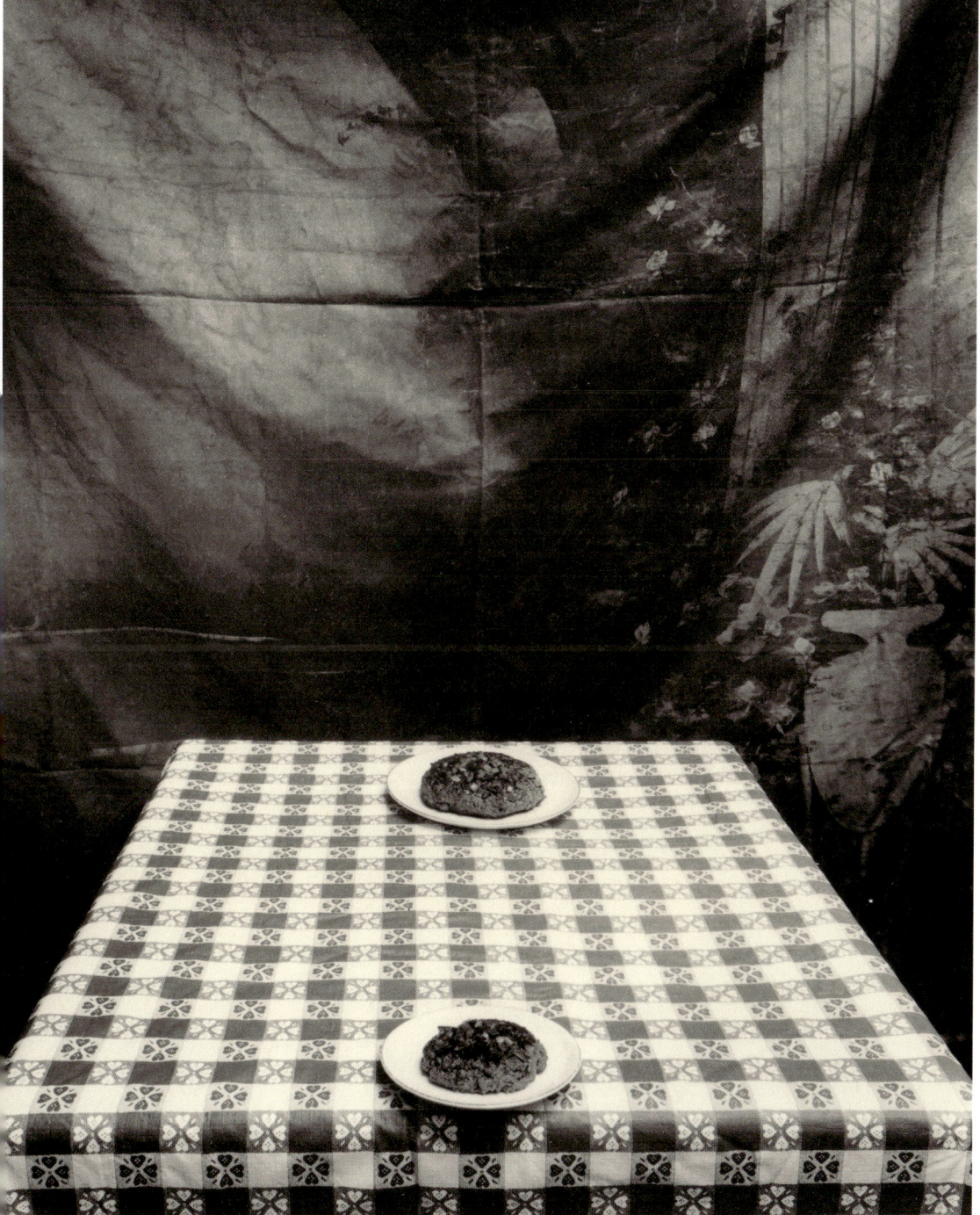

4) Remove the patties to a warm platter, and, to the skillet, add 1 tablespoon of the butter and the chopped green onions. Cook until the onions are wilted, stirring with a wooden spoon. Add the white wine, and cook for another minute. Add the broth and the lemon juice and cook until reduced to about 4 tablespoons. Add the Slivovitz and remove from heat. Swirl in the remaining tablespoon of butter.

5) Return the patties to the skillet, and turn them once without cooking.

Serve with sauce, and garnish with chopped parsley.

Les Krims's Formalist Stew

I've got a great recipe for "Formalist Stew."

It has 185 ingredients and takes 31 days to prepare. The only problem is, you die of hunger and boredom before it's ever finished.

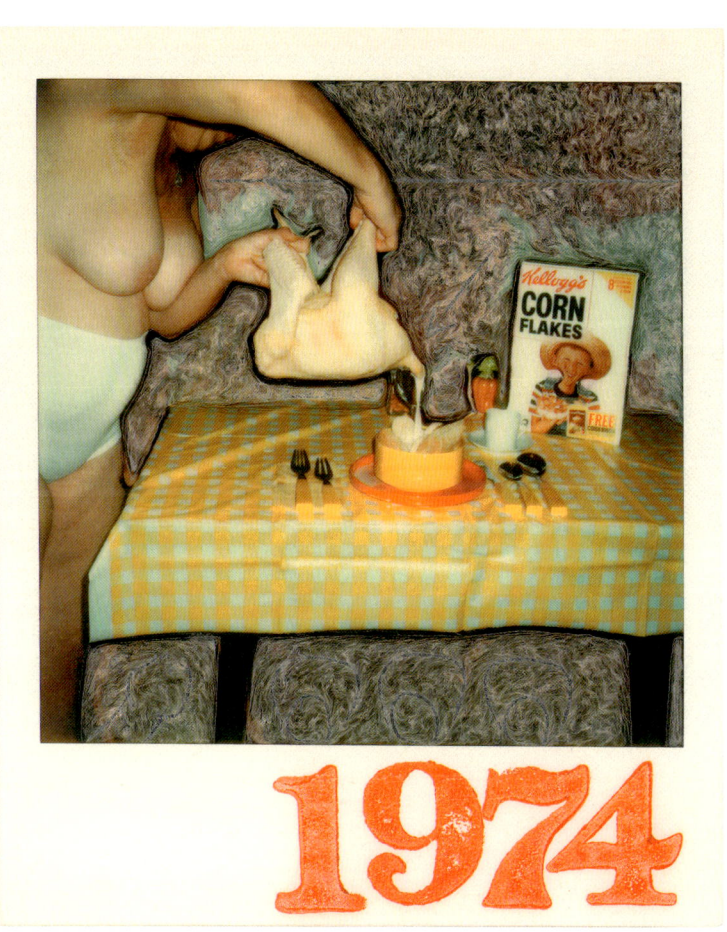

1974

Arthur Rothstein's Gai Lo Sze Tien

I lived and worked in China from 1944 to 1946. In World War II, I was the U.S. Army Photo Officer there, later Chief Photographer for United Nations Relief Rehabilitation Administration.

Gai is chicken. Lo Sze Tien is my name in phonetic Mandarin, and it means "Scholar Seeking High."

½ chicken
1 onion
2 tablespoons sesame oil
1 teaspoon five spices
    (blend of anise,
    cinnamon, cloves,
    ginger, and nutmeg,
    which is commonly
    sold in Asian food
    markets)
1 clove garlic
1 teaspoon curry powder

2 teaspoons salt
1 teaspoon sugar
1-inch piece of fresh
    ginger root,
    chopped fine
2 green peppers cut into
    bite-size pieces
½ cup white wine
3 cups bean sprouts
½ cup sliced
    water chestnuts
Cellophane noodles

Cut chicken through bones into bite-size pieces. Sauté onions 2 minutes in well-greased wok. Remove onions—add 2 tablespoons sesame oil to wok. Sauté chicken—3 minutes with spices. Add wine, sugar, salt, garlic—cover, simmer for 10 minutes. Turn heat high—add vegetables. When boiling—lower heat—cover, cook 2 minutes. Serve with cellophane noodles.

Serves 2–4.

70   Arthur Rothstein, Housewives Killing a Chicken for Dinner, Decatur Homesteads, Indiana, 1938

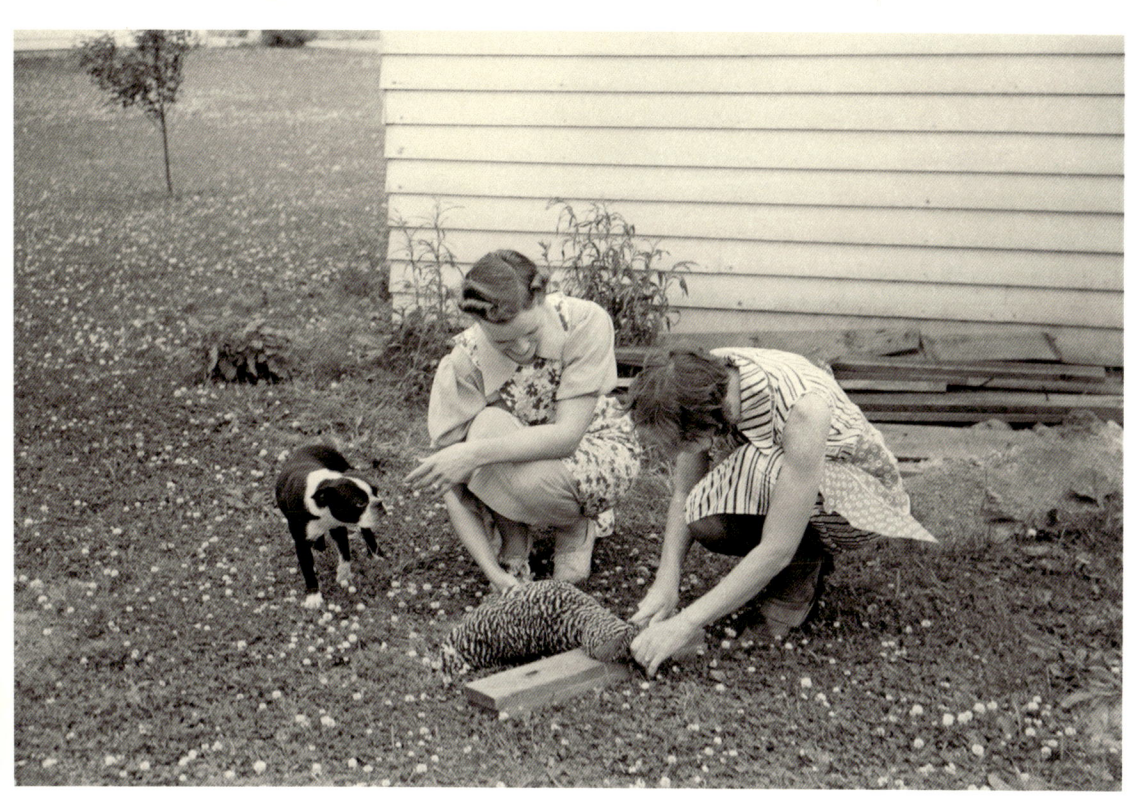

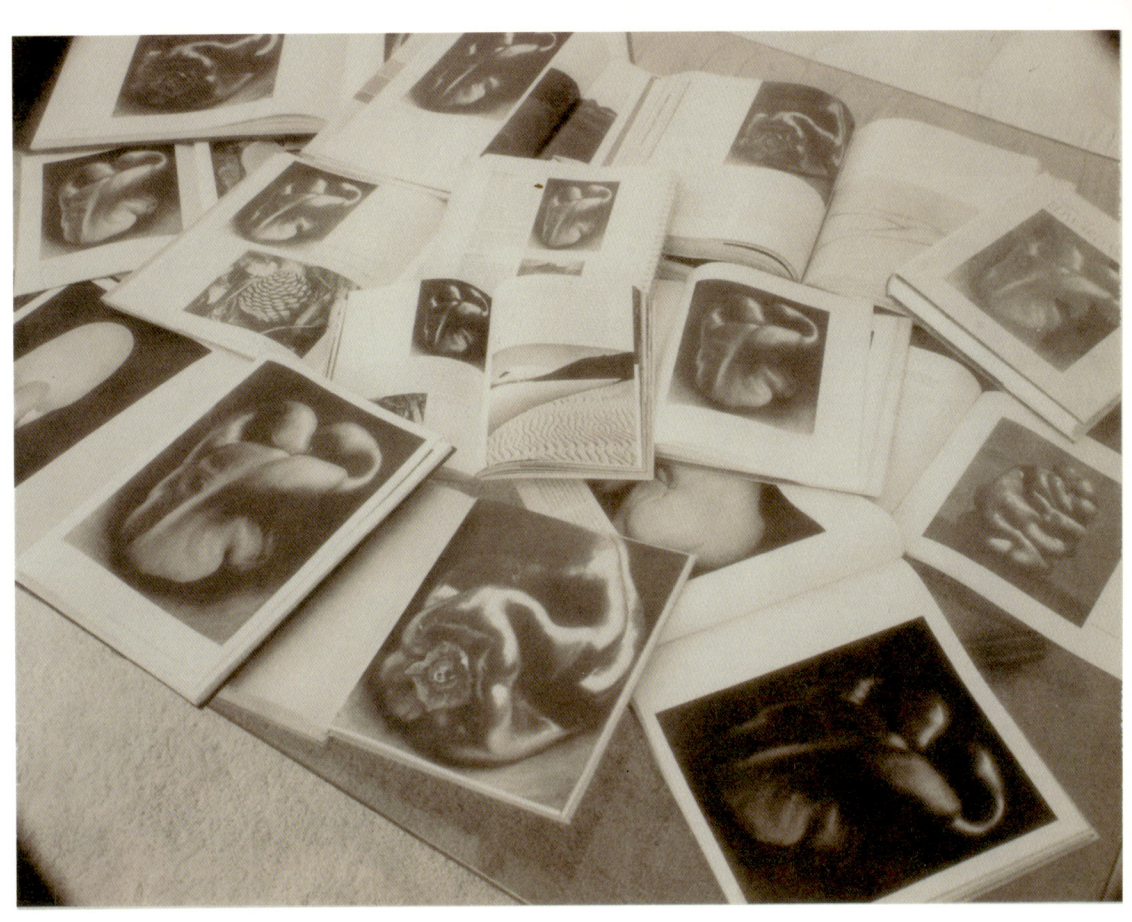

Arthur Taussig's Tongue in "Polish" Sauce with Crouton and Apricot Dumplings

Three from the land of Josef Sudek. My parents are from Czechoslovakia, and I have many fond childhood memories of unspeakably wonderful sauces and dumplings, cakes, and tortes. As Sudek's photographs are unashamedly romantic, thick in Bohemian atmosphere, so are these dishes; they are not dietetic. I have made translations of the titles; since several letters have no English equivalents the names become unpronounceable, and the saying becomes more difficult than the cooking.

Tongue in "Polish" Sauce

In a medium-size pot, cook 4 pounds of lamb or veal tongues in cold water covered with 2 carrots, broken into pieces, a handful of celery tops, and a few sprigs of parsley. Bring to a boil, cover, and cook until tender. If you are unfamiliar with cooking tongue, use a meat fork to test the tenderness of the meat. When done, remove the tongues with a slotted spoon, reserve the liquid, and rinse the tongues in cold water until cool enough to handle. Peel the skin from the tongues, remove any fat from the backs, and slice thinly.

In a saucepan, sauté ½ onion, 1 carrot, ½ celery root, and 1 celery stalk all finely chopped, in 2 tablespoons butter. When slightly softened, sprinkle with about 2 tablespoons flour, and continue sautéing until color begins to appear. Add 1 cup tightly packed brown sugar, 8 peppercorns, juice of a medium lemon, ¼ cup dry white wine, 8 cloves, and ⅓ cup grated ginger bread. Add 6 cups of the reserved stock, bring to a boil, and simmer

73   Arthur Taussig, Books with reproductions
      of Weston's pepper, 1979

1 hour. Pass through a sieve, pressing the liquid from any solids, and add 3 dozen blanched almonds, ½ cup raisins, and the grated peel of a lemon. If necessary, thicken slightly with a roux. Add fine cider vinegar to taste (a ½ cup is about right). Add tongue, heat, and serve with crouton dumplings (recipe below). Freezes well.

Serves 8.

Crouton Dumplings

Cut 8 slices of white or French bread into crouton shapes, and brown slowly in butter or oil in a large pan, turning occasionally so that all sides are evenly browned. In a small dish combine ½ package dry yeast, 1 tablespoon sugar, and ½ cup warm milk. Set aside in warm area to proof. Combine yeast mixture with 3 cups flour, 1⅓ cups cream of wheat, 2 eggs, and 1 cup water. Mix thoroughly using a wooden spoon. Fold in about 2 cups croutons. Cover the mixing bowl with a damp towel and allow to rise (double in size) in a warm place. Bring 8 quarts of salted water to boil. Shape the dumplings using wet hands (so that the dough will not stick to your hands) into 3 or 4 loaf shapes. Place the dumplings gently into the boiling water. Boil for 20 minutes, turning occasionally. Remove with a large slotted spoon and cut into 1-inch-thick slices using a strong cotton thread (knives will tear the dumplings).* Can be made in advance and heated in a steamer before use.

Serves 8.

* The dumpling is placed on a cutting board, the thread
is placed under the dumpling, the ends are crossed over the
dumpling, and the thread is pulled—much like a garrote.

Apricot Dumplings

The following is not a dessert but used as a meal.

Combine 2½ cups flour, 1 egg, 1 tablespoon softened butter,
and 1 pound low-fat, small-curd cottage cheese drained of any
liquid. Mix with hands, and add more flour if necessary until
the dough no longer adheres to the mixing bowl or board. Use
the dough to wrap thinly (about ½-inch-thick) apricots whose
stones have been removed. Makes about 20 dumplings. Using
a slotted spoon, gently lower the dumplings into boiling, lightly
salted water. Make sure they do not stick to the bottom of
the pot. Boil 7 minutes; they should float when done. Remove
carefully with a slotted spoon. Pierce each dumpling with
a fork. Serve hot in a bowl. Each diner takes as many dumplings
as desired. They are quartered, sprinkled with grated farmer
cheese, sugar, and brown butter. Other fruits can be substituted
for apricots: cherries with stones removed (use 3 per dumpling),
plums, or strawberries. These dumplings will freeze moderately
well, wrapped separately in foil. They lose some textural
properties, but in the middle of winter no one cares.

* To make brown butter: In a small saucepan slowly simmer
½ pound sweet butter for about 2 hours. It should attain
a dark color. Do not discard any solids that form—these are
considered delicacies.

Jerry Uelsmann's Shrimp Apple Curry

½ cup water
1 (13-ounce) can
    evaporated milk
¼ cup flaked coconut
2 apples
3 tablespoons butter
⅓ cup onion, minced
½ cup celery,
    thinly sliced
¼ cup raisins
3 cups fresh shrimp
2½ teaspoons curry powder
1 clove garlic, minced

1 teaspoon salt
¼ teaspoon white pepper
3 tablespoons flour
2 tablespoons lemon juice
Cooked rice

Chopped peanuts (optional)
Fruit chutney (optional)

Selection of condiments:
    shredded coconut,
    almonds, raisins,
    tomatoes (optional)

Combine water and milk, pour over coconut, and let stand 30 minutes to make coconut milk. Peel and core apples, chop coarsely. Melt butter in skillet or wok. Sauté onion, celery, and raisins until tender. Add apples, shrimp, curry powder, garlic, salt, and white pepper. Cook over moderate heat until apples are just tender. Sprinkle with flour and stir in. Add coconut milk and lemon juice. Cook, stirring constantly until mixture boils and thickens.

Serve over hot rice and top with chopped peanuts. Accompany with a fresh fruit chutney and a selection of condiments (coconut, almonds, raisins, tomatoes, etc.).

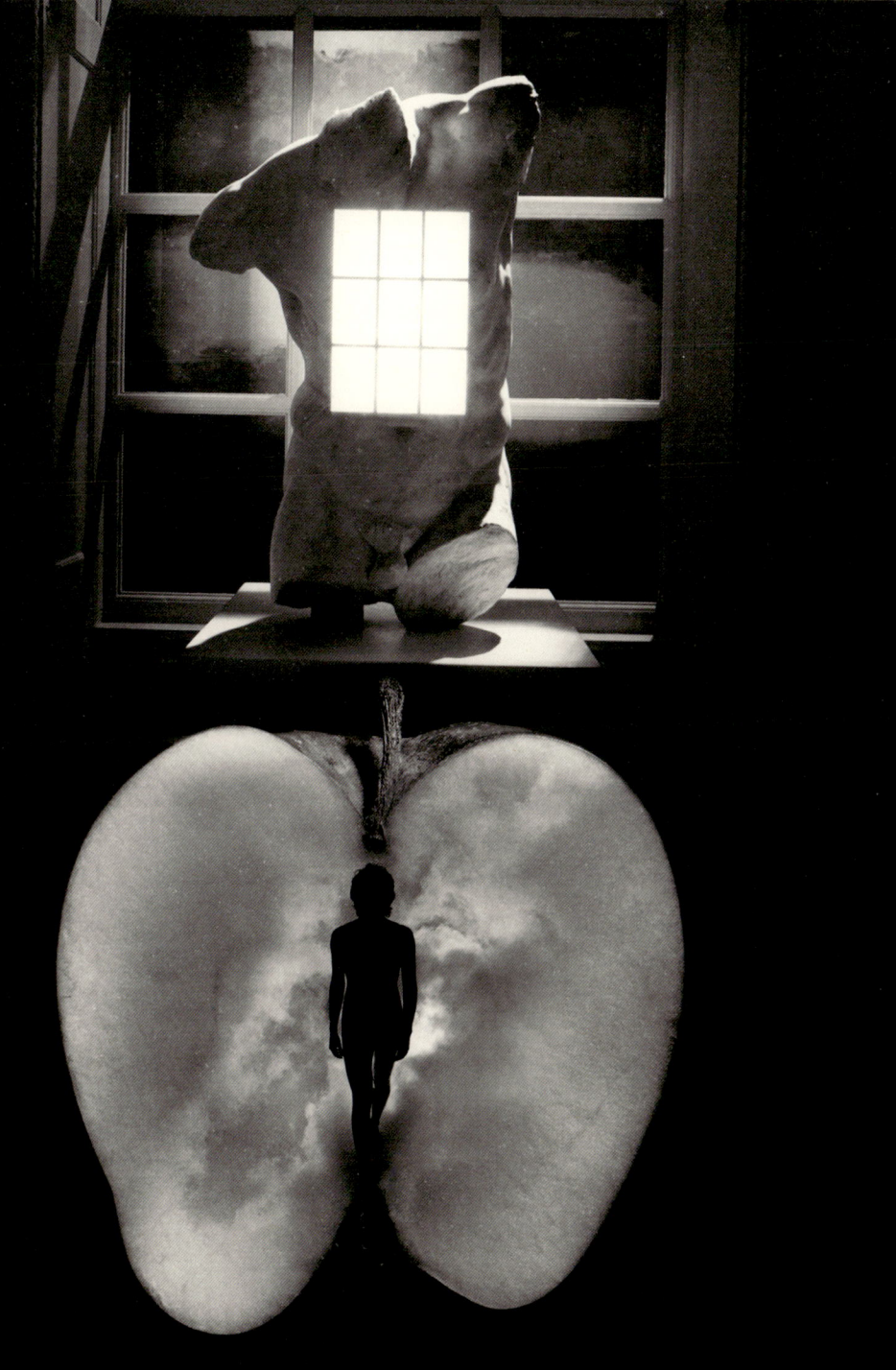

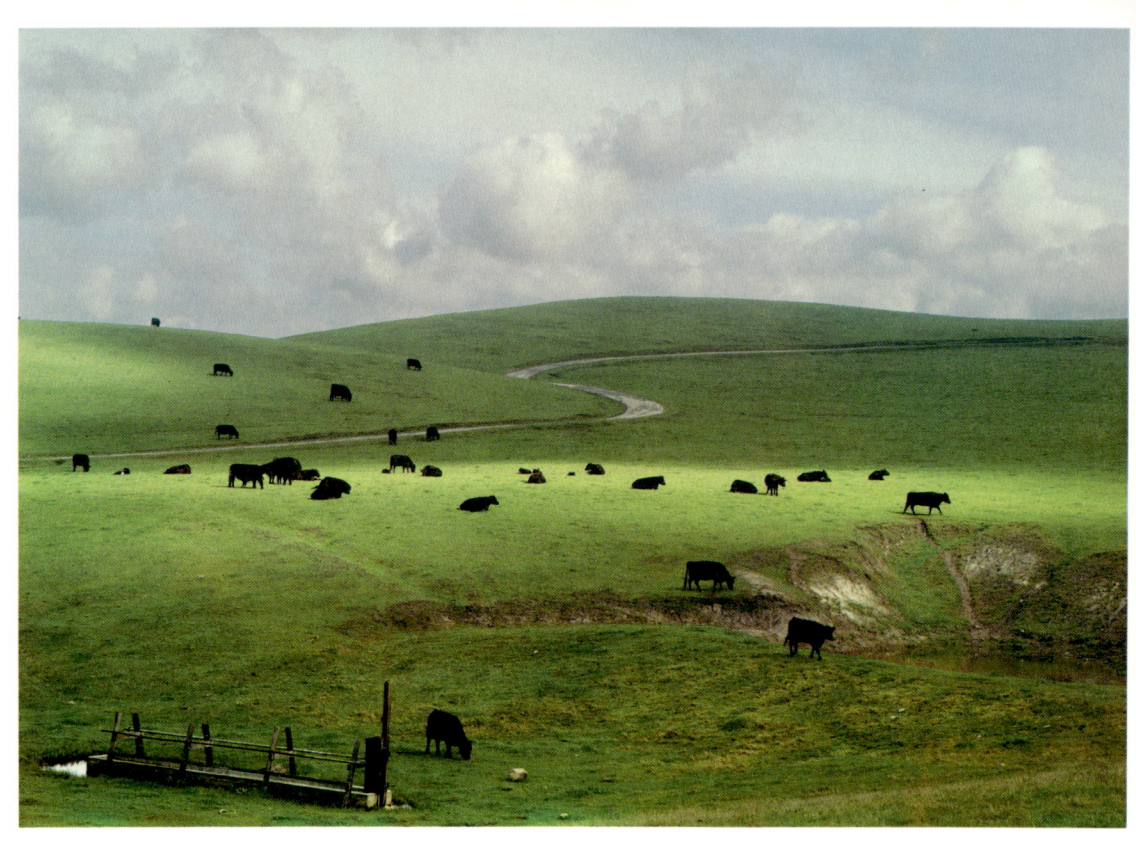

Cole Weston's California Beef and Barley

1 pound ground beef
1 onion, diced
1 cup chopped green pepper
1 clove garlic, minced
Salt to taste
Pepper to taste
1 large can (16-ounce) tomatoes
2 tablespoons chili powder
1 teaspoon ground cumin
1 teaspoon oregano
1 cup pearl barley
1½ cups water
1 cup raisins
8 large pita (pocket) breads
Yogurt

Brown ground beef with onion, green pepper, garlic, salt, and pepper. Add canned tomatoes, including liquid, and add spices. Stir in barley and water, and allow to simmer, covered, for 35–40 minutes. Add raisins just before serving to allow them to plump up. Cut pita bread in half, and fill each pocket with the mixture. Garnish with globs of yogurt.

Serves 8.

79   Cole Weston, Palo Corona Ranch,
        1962

Vegetables

Eileen Cowin's Vegetable Cheese Casserole

There is a scene in Even Cowgirls Get the Blues by Tom Robbins where someone sprays a special substance on different foods to make them taste like chocolate chip cookies. That would be my favorite recipe if I could find it. Since I haven't . . .

Sauté in very little oil: onions, mushrooms, broccoli, tomatoes. (You can substitute any combination of vegetables in any amounts.)

Add spices/herbs: garlic, salt, pepper, basil. (Again, changing or adding different combinations makes the dish taste different every time you make it.)

Sauté vegetables until they are a little tender, remove from stove, and put into a casserole dish.

Mix ricotta cheese (1 cup ricotta to 3 cups vegetables or according to your taste) with salt, pepper, parsley, and egg (1 egg per cup of cheese). Add ricotta mixture to vegetables. Bake at 350 degrees for 25 minutes.

The last 5 minutes, put thinly sliced mozzarella cheese over the top of the casserole.

I hope this isn't too loose, but the best part of this is making up your own variations. And, if you want, you can find that special substance mentioned above, and make the whole thing taste like a chocolate chip cookie.

82   Eileen Cowin, Untitled (Boy with TV),
        1980; from the series Family Docudrama

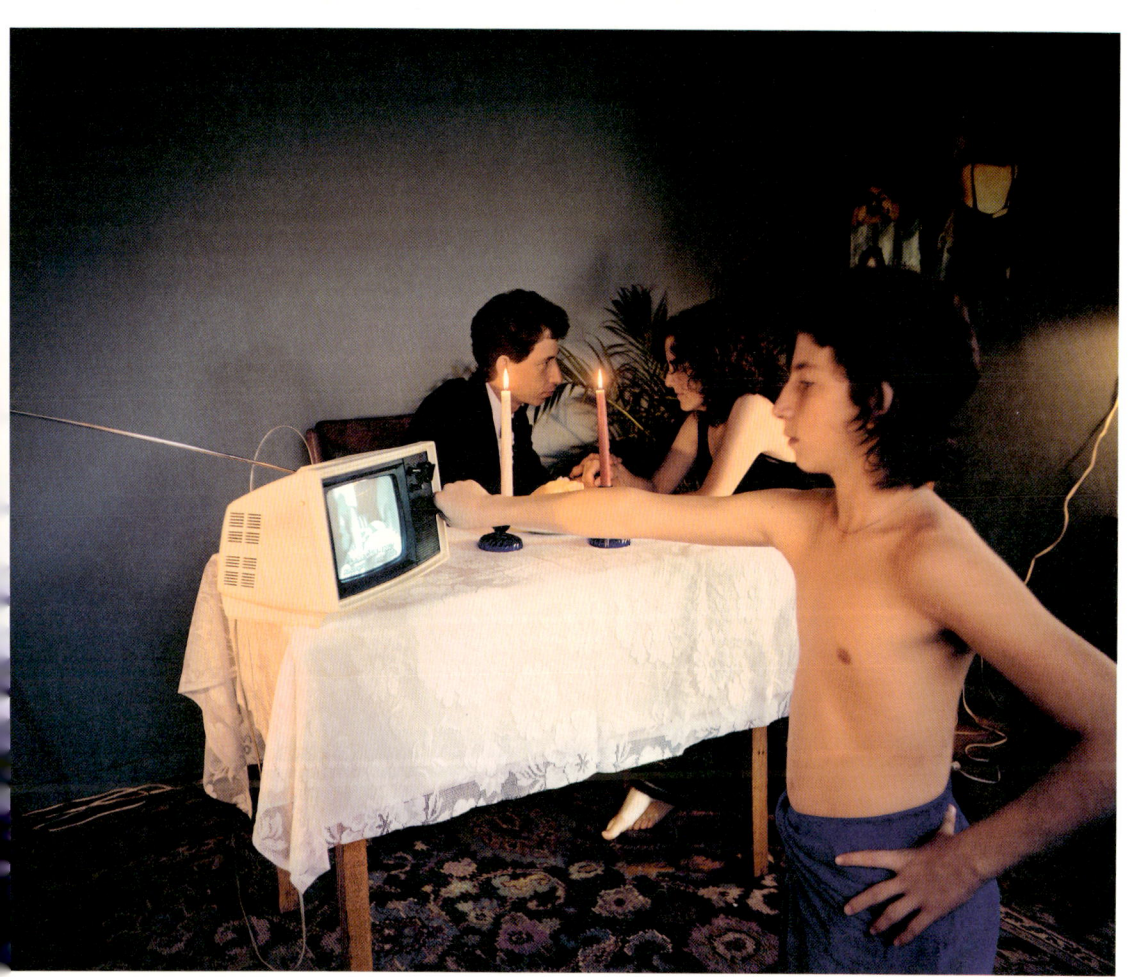

Horst P. Horst's Cucumber Salad

Generally I like simple food:
grilled fish or meat; boiled potatoes;
fresh, slightly undercooked
vegetables; fresh fruit. No sauces.

Marinate cucumbers, sliced very
thin, in salt for at least 1 hour.
The cucumbers have to be squeezed
nearly dry. Add dill, chopped, and
sour cream.

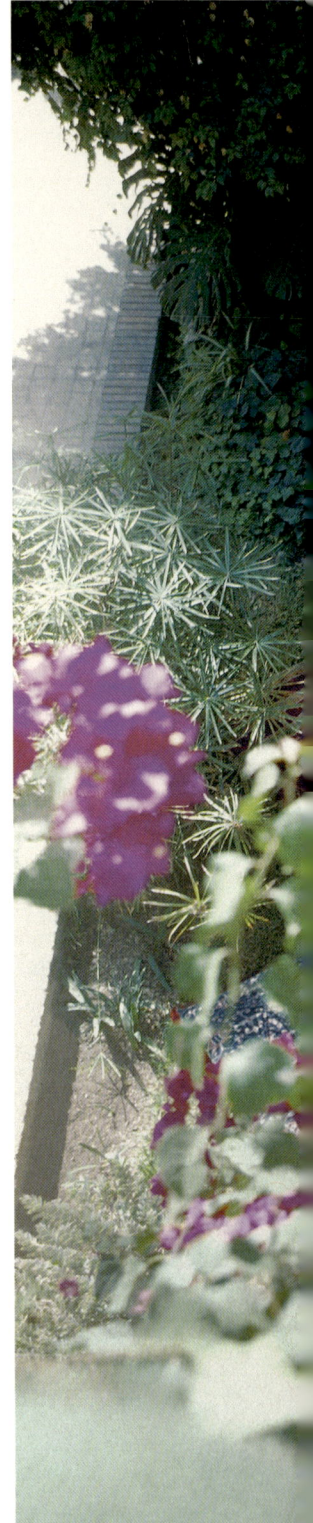

84   Horst P. Horst, Yves Saint Laurent
      in His Garden, 1986

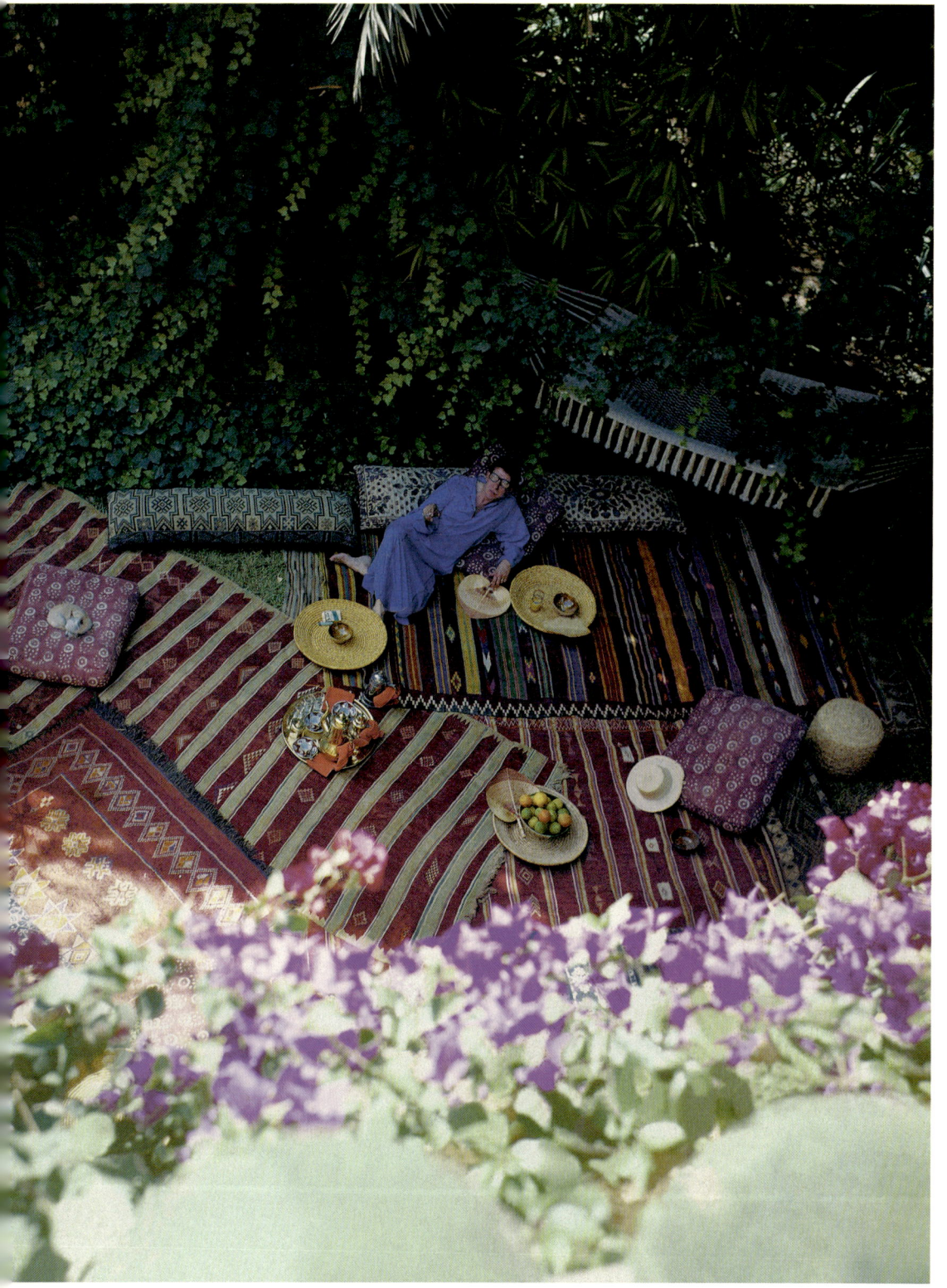

Beaumont Newhall's Choucroute Luncheon for Mr. James Beard

It was our pleasure last week to cook luncheon for Mr. James Beard, the eminent gastronome and master craftsman who was in Rochester demonstrating the fine art of cooking at the Museum of Arts and Sciences.

Four sat down to luncheon at our home: Mr. Beard; Mr. W. Stephen Thomas, director of the Rochester Museum and Science Center; Mr. William Gamble, president of the Rochester Museum Association; and your reporter.

The menu consisted entirely of "Epicure Corner" recipes: salted almonds with cocktails, choucroute garnie, parsley potatoes, tossed green salad, caramel custard, and Italian coffee (espresso).

Naturally, the prospect of cooking for so gastronomically illustrious a guest was somewhat worrisome; the challenge was great. But Mr. Beard was most gracious. The ice was brokenwhen one of the guests asked, "What is 'Choucroute?'" We explained as simply as we could:

Finely shred a head of cabbage, wash it well in several changes of water, and then put it in a deep pot with 1 cup of tarragon red wine vinegar. Let it steep overnight. In the morning wash it again and add 1 cup of beef stock and 12 peppercorns. Cover the mound of cabbage with, for each guest, 2 pieces each of Canadian bacon, cooked ham, and Italian salami. Simmer over a gentle heat for 2 hours.

86   Beaumont Newhall, Edward Weston's Kitchen, 1940

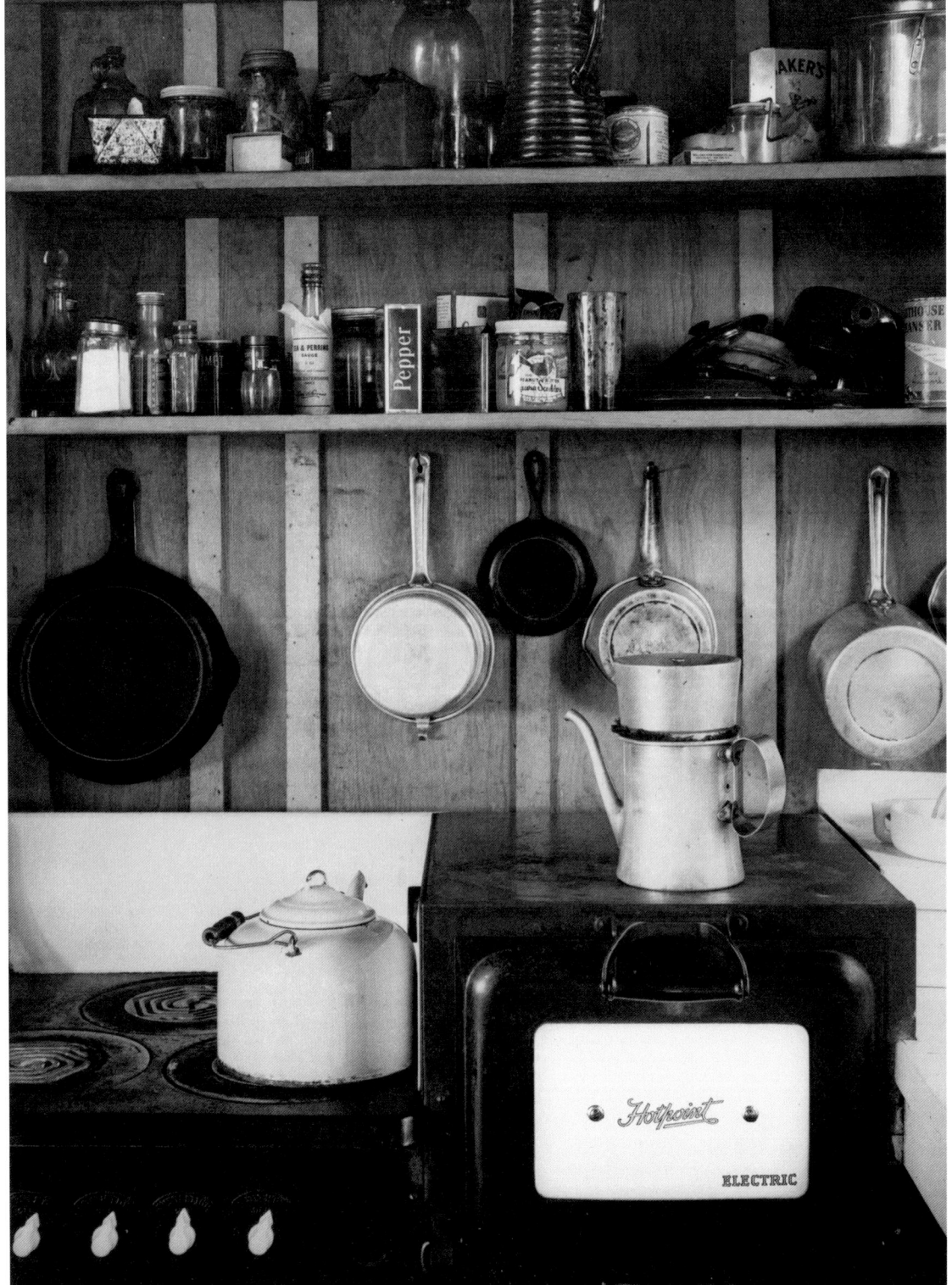

When we finished our description Mr. Beard nodded his head
in approval—and took the second of three helpings he enjoyed.
No greater compliment could be shown.

We sent the "Choucroute" to the table in a large Scandinavian
casserole with the meat decoratively placed in the middle.
Around the edges of the casserole we placed the parsley
potatoes. When we served it we removed all the meat to a side
dish and then piled cabbage on each guest's plate and covered
it with pieces of meat and laid a couple of potatoes to one side.

Two varieties of mustard—Dijon and Düsseldorf—were passed.
There was a loaf of French bread on the cutting board with
a knife freshly sharpened for the occasion.

The wine was Pouilly-Fuisse of fresh vintage (1964),
well chilled.

Naturally, we talked shop with Mr. Beard. We asked him if he
had the same problem we have faced ever since we started this
column nine years ago: the apparent intimidation of the very
people we want to help—hosts and especially hostesses who
almost universally complain that they don't dare cook for us.

"Oh, yes!" he replied. "I'm practically a social outcast!"

"Do people say that your recipes are complicated?"

"Invariably," he replied. "But the worst thing is when they
ask you for substitutes. Today, a lady asked me what to use in
place of nutmeg. 'Mace,' I replied—but I didn't explain that
mace is the husk of nutmeg."

Arnold Newman:
Nina's Cottage Cheese Salad

On one of my periodic diets and while photographing Nina Foch,
she prepared the following diet luncheon salad for me, which
I can stomach. Since I have been on and off diets practically
from the age of two, I find this tasty, tangy salad satisfies my
lunch-time hunger—almost.

>   2 large radishes
>   ¼ medium-size green pepper
>   ¾ cup fat-free cottage cheese
>   Hot mustard to taste
>   Salt to taste
>   Ground black pepper to taste
>   Ground nutmeg

Cut radishes and green pepper into small pieces and
mix with cottage cheese. Blend mustard, salt, and pepper into
mixture, and garnish with nutmeg. Makes a heaping portion
for lunch.

89   Arnold Newman, Julia Child Portrait,
     1970

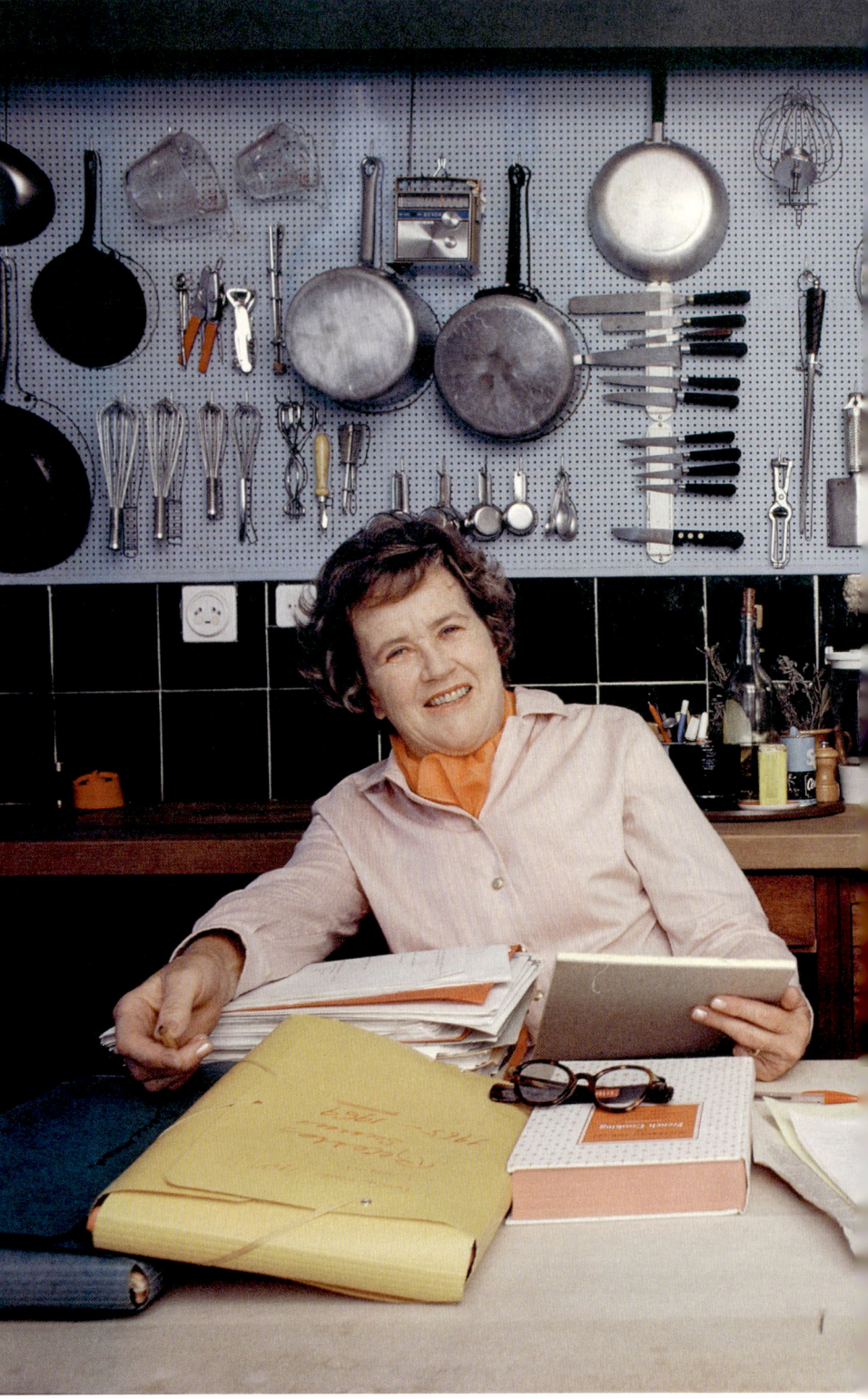

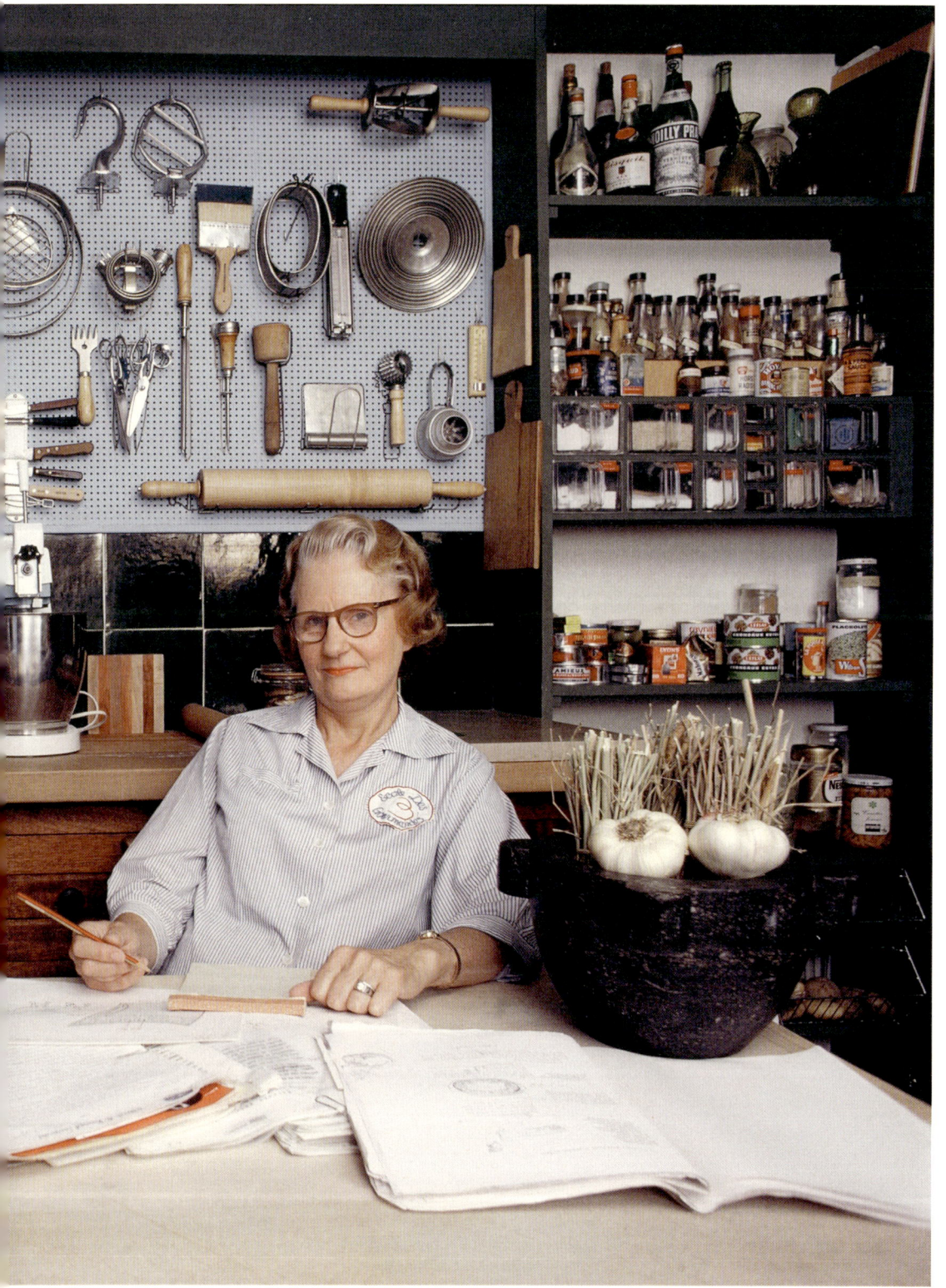

Arthur Tress's Sweet and Sour Broccoli

1 bunch broccoli, chopped
2 cups dried apples, chopped
1 cup raisins (red and/or white—use your imagination)
½ cup coarsely chopped onions

Steam or simmer the ingredients above for 6–10 minutes, until tender.

Make dressing of 3 parts peanut oil, 1 part cider vinegar, a dash or two of sesame oil, basil to taste.

Sprinkle the whole dish with chopped walnuts.

A great conversation dish at parties or at home alone when you've no one to talk to.

92   Arthur Tress, Nursing the "Dog," Playland, San Francisco, 1964

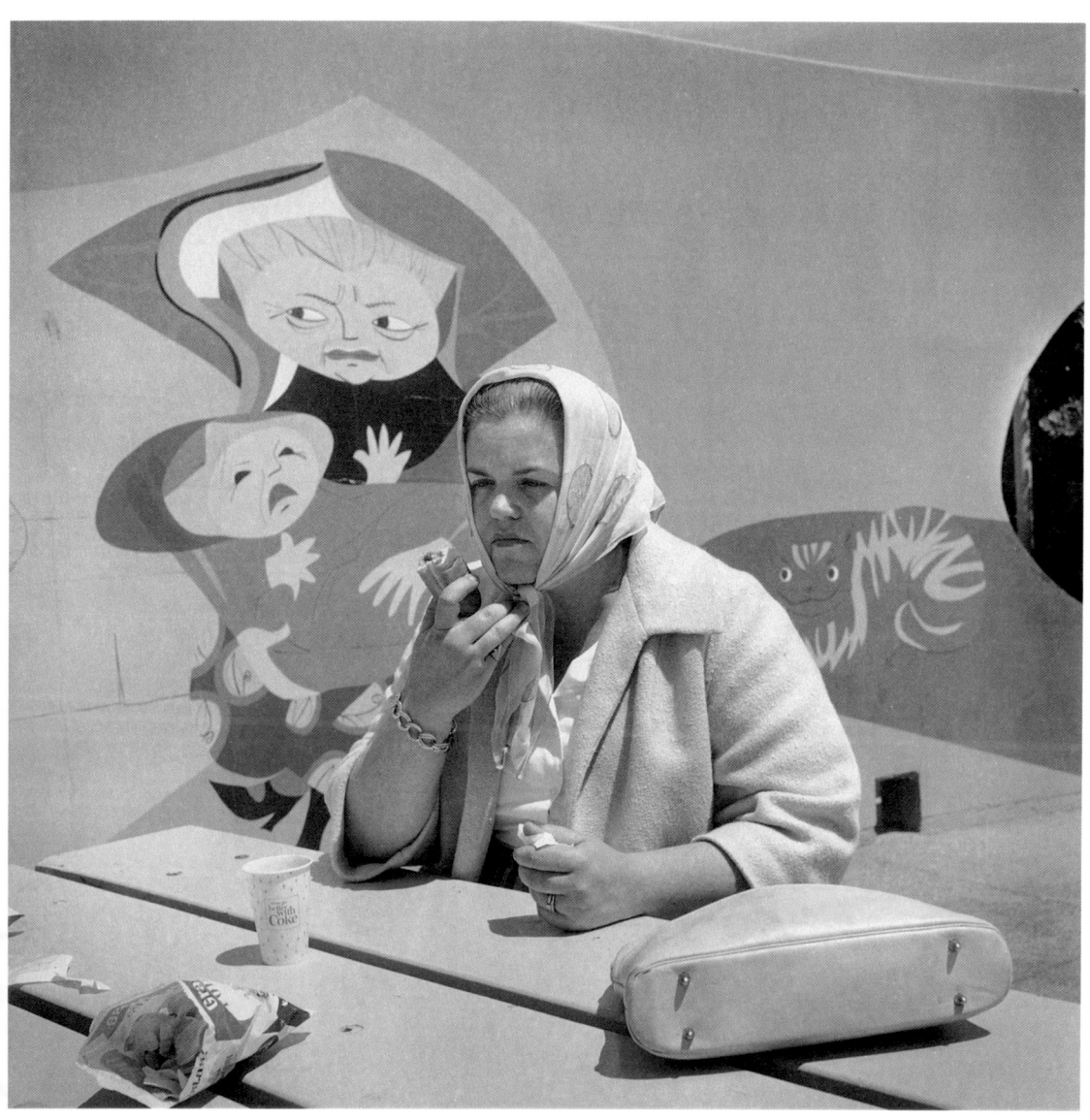

Minor White's Steamed and Sautéed Vegetables

The ritual performance of the process from conception to final assembly in book or exhibition is sought at all times. Heightened awareness occurs and is brought to bear at 1) exposure, 2) printing, 3) editing photos into sequences, groups, exhibitions, articles, etc.

During editing, heightened awareness is invoked frequently whenever choices must be made until final result satisfies, then the threads of weaving several separate photos are broken.

Seen as a whole, the production of a sequence with words is a complex tapestry indeed.

Ingredients:
Carrots, celery, zucchini, onions

As variants: string beans, cauliflower, mushrooms, or anything that is in the icebox that appeals to you

Slice or dice carrots and celery and place in steamer first. Steam for 6 minutes. Add chopped onion and sliced zucchini and steam for 3 minutes. Have ready a frying pan with a very small amount of oil, preferably safflower oil or soybean oil, and pour the steamed vegetables into the frying pan which is very hot, stir briskly. Add 2 tablespoons of tamari sauce, stir, and cover and let steam for about 1 minute. This whole operation should take approximately 3 minutes. Serve at once.

94   Minor White, San Mateo County, California, 1947

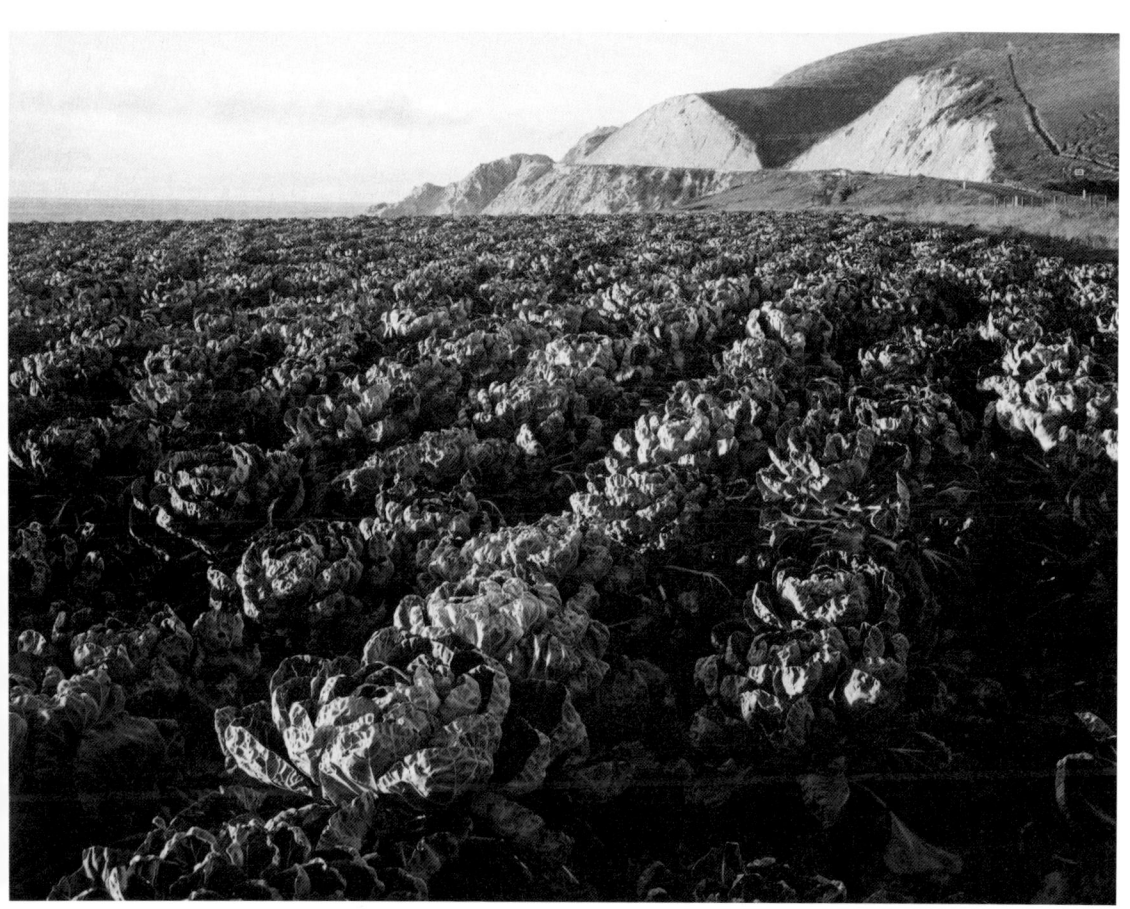

Variations are endless. A pound of spinach steamed the last
1 minute is one way. If string beans are used, they should go
in with the carrots and celery. Cauliflower, the same.

Quantities can be estimated for the number of people
to be served. It can be used as a main dish or as a side dish.

Breads & Starches

Peter Bunnell's Riz à la Portugaise

A taste for superb cuisine is fundamental to a full, authentic, and varied life. An artist, critic, or historian who lacks an appreciation of good food and drink has only a negligible chance of revealing in his work any significant interpretation of human understanding. The culinary arts themselves are a lesson in the pure elegance of aesthetic creation.

Here is a recipe for a dish I frequently serve, sometimes to large groups. It is an adaptation of a recipe by Paul Poiret, French fashion designer and chef, who, in 1928, published a marvelous cookbook entitled 107 Recettes ou Curiosités Culinaires Recueillies par Poiret.

¼ pound sliced bacon, cut into ½-inch lengths	1 cup peeled, seeded, diced tomato
½ cup chopped onion	6 sprigs parsley
½ cup chopped green pepper	1 bay leaf
2½ cups raw converted (parboiled) rice	½ teaspoon thyme
½ cup sliced black olives	Freshly ground pepper
	4¾ cups water
	2 teaspoons salt

1) Preheat oven to 375 degrees.

2) In a large, heavy saucepan, sauté the bacon for 2–3 minutes or until it renders some of its fat. Add the onion and green pepper and cook the mixture, stirring occasionally, until the onion is soft and translucent.

Jim McQuaid, Untitled, 1977

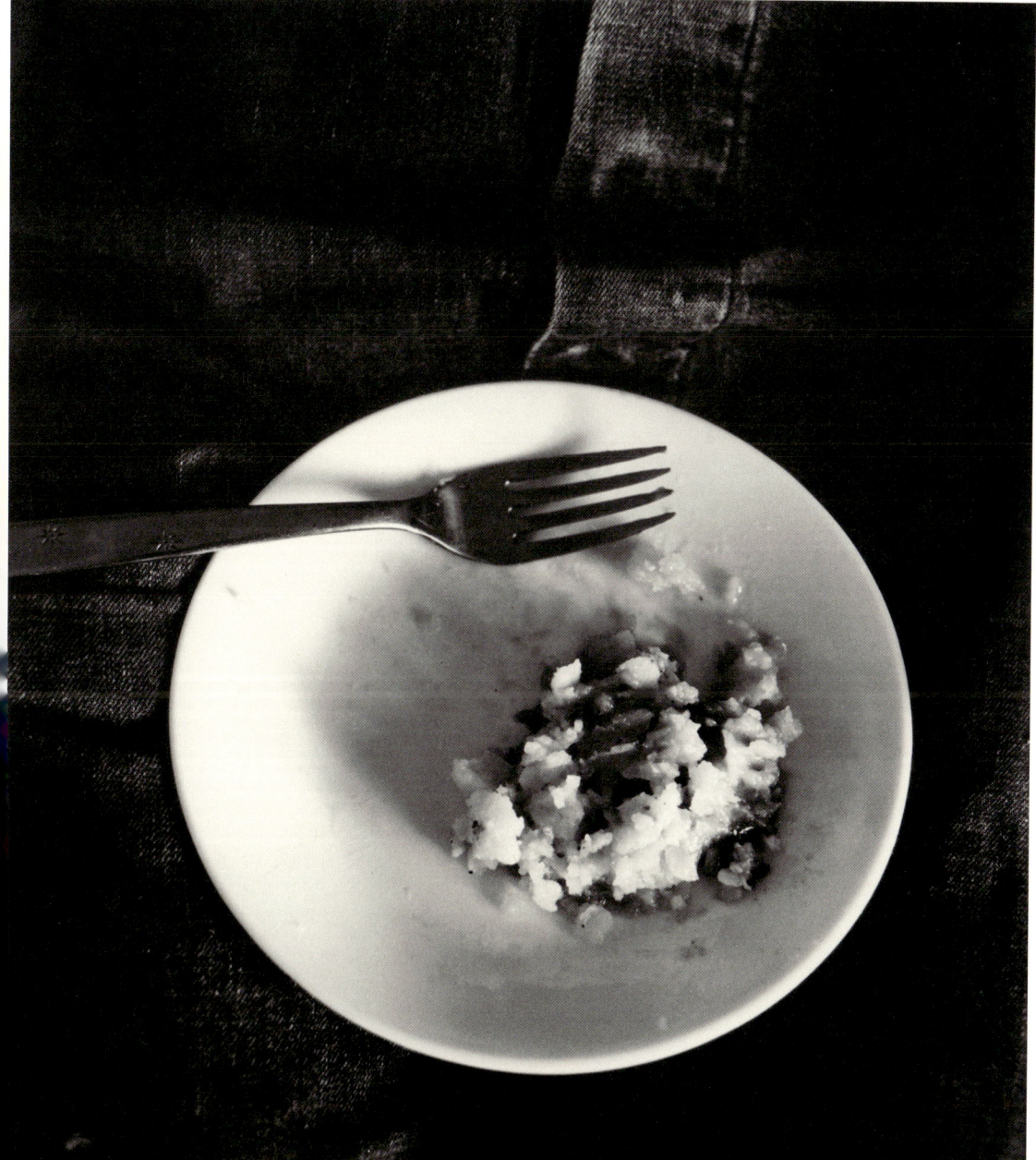

3)   Add the rice and stir it with a fork for 2 minutes to coat
     it with the fat. Tie the olives, tomato, parsley, and bay leaf
     in a bouquet garni. Add bouquet garni to the bacon, onion,
     and green pepper mixture. Then add the thyme and ground
     pepper to taste. Pour in the water and add the salt. Bring the
     mixture to a boil, stirring constantly to avoid scorching.

4)   As soon as the mixture boils, cover the pan tightly with
     the lid and bake for 20 minutes or until the rice is tender.
     Remove the bouquet garni, and fluff the rice with a fork.

Serves 10–12.

Marion Faller's Nut Loaf with Variations

Have all ingredients at room temperature. With an electric
beater, mix together the following, liquids first:

> ½ cup safflower or other vegetable oil
> ½ cup honey
> 1 large egg
> 1¾ cups whole-wheat flour
> ¼ cup wheat germ or bran
> 2 teaspoons baking powder

Choose and make 1 of the following mixtures to create the main
flavors of the bread:

—   1 cup unsweetened applesauce, 1 cup raisins, 1 teaspoon
    cinnamon, ½ teaspoon cloves

- 1 cup steamed pumpkin or other winter squash, 1 teaspoon cinnamon, ½ teaspoon nutmeg, ¼ teaspoon ginger, ½ teaspoon cloves, ¼ cup milk
- 1 cup grated raw zucchini or other summer squash (unpeeled), 1 teaspoon vanilla, 1 teaspoon cinnamon, ¼ teaspoon nutmeg, ¼ cup milk
- 2 large ripe mashed bananas, ¼ teaspoon freshly grated nutmeg
- 1 cup pitted dates (firmly packed), ¾ cup boiling water, 1 teaspoon vanilla
- 1 cup raisins, ½ cup milk, 1 tablespoon vanilla, 1 teaspoon allspice
- 1 cup raisins, ½ cup milk, 1 tablespoon vanilla, 1 teaspoon allspice
- 1 cup unsweetened crushed pineapple, drained, 1 teaspoon freshly ground coriander, grated rind of ½ lemon
- 1 cup grated raw carrots, 1 teaspoon cinnamon, ½ teaspoon freshly grated nutmeg, 6 ounces plain yogurt
- ½ cup skim milk, then gently fold in 1½ cups fresh blueberries coated with a few tablespoons flour

To the chosen mixture, add 1 cup chopped nuts (walnuts, raw cashews, pecans, etc.) and/or unsalted sunflower seeds. Put into oiled loaf pan. Sprinkle with seeds (sesame, poppy, celery, etc.). Bake in preheated 350-degree oven for approximately 40 minutes. Cool before cutting. Store in refrigerator. Makes 1 loaf (although this recipe doubles, triples, etc., very well).

After you have tried some of these variations, make up your own. Some possibilities: raw rhubarb, fresh or dried peaches or apricots, orange rind, etc.

101   Marion Faller and Hollis Frampton, 33. Zucchini Squash Encountering Sawhorse, 1975; from the series Sixteen Studies from Vegetable Locomotion

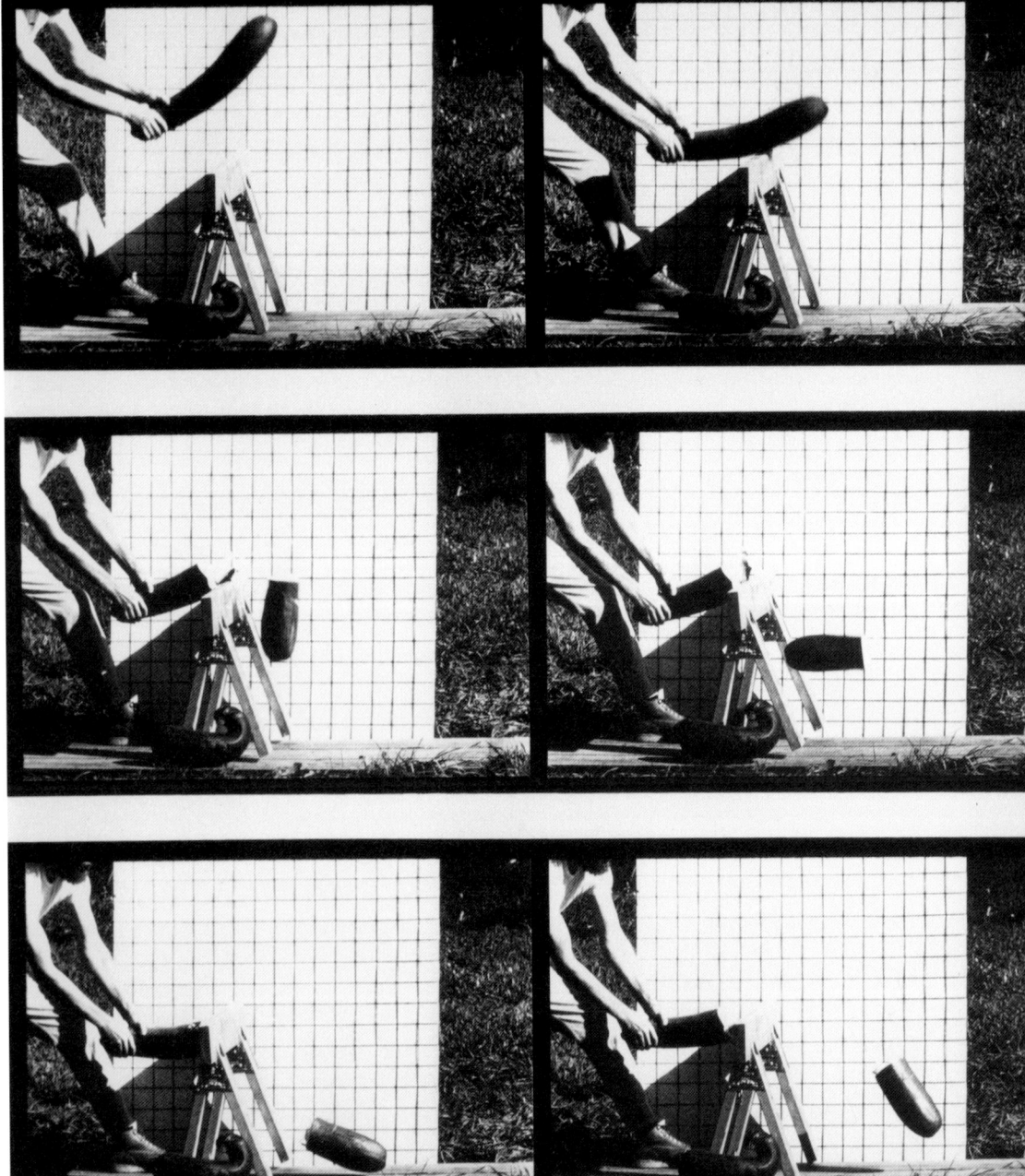

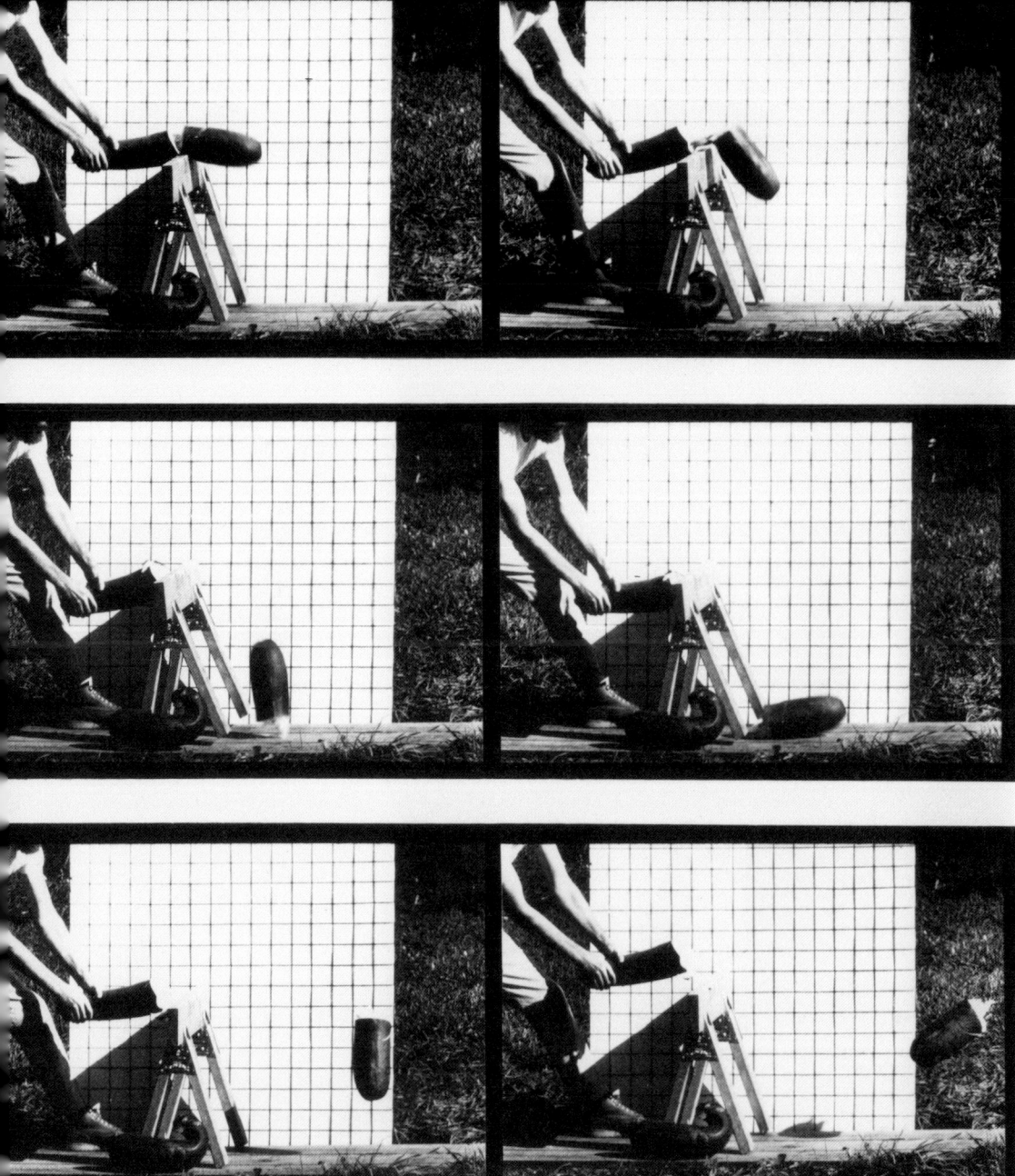

David Freund's Potato-Onion Underlay with Variations

My one food photograph, and therefore my recipe, has fish in it. But my first idea, a simple, nourishing foil ball of baked fish, onion, and potato, lacked, perhaps, vertigo. Reading complicated recipes, however, makes the evening news hard to follow; so, I submit a dish I think still simple, but variable, maybe describable as a systems approach to supper. It works if you're eating alone or with several. The description is for one; multiply as necessary.

Step 1 is always:

1)   Slice a serving's worth of potato and onion, about ¼-inch thick. Salt and pepper.

2)   Bake in greased, covered pan with ¼ cup water at 425 degrees for 45 minutes.

Step 2 is variable. Three variations I like are:

Fish:

Sprinkle the potatoes and onion of step 1 with a little tarragon and disperse a slice of bacon, diced, on top. Cook. When done, add ¼ cup dry white wine and cover with a serving of fish fillet, seasoned with salt, pepper, and tarragon. Bake, covered, an additional 10–15 minutes.

Chicken:

    Sauté a clove or 2 of garlic and some mushrooms in butter, and stir into step 1 while it's cooking. Brown in the skillet a serving of boned chicken breast, seasoned with salt, pepper, and tarragon (or almost any other herb). After step 1 has cooked 30 minutes, add ¼ cup dry sherry, place chicken on top, and bake an additional 20 minutes.

Kielbasy:

    After step 1, cover with slices of kielbasy and cook an additional 10 minutes.

Step 3 is optional, but I favor covering the dish with some harmonious cheese, such as Jarlsberg, and melting it either in the oven or broiler.

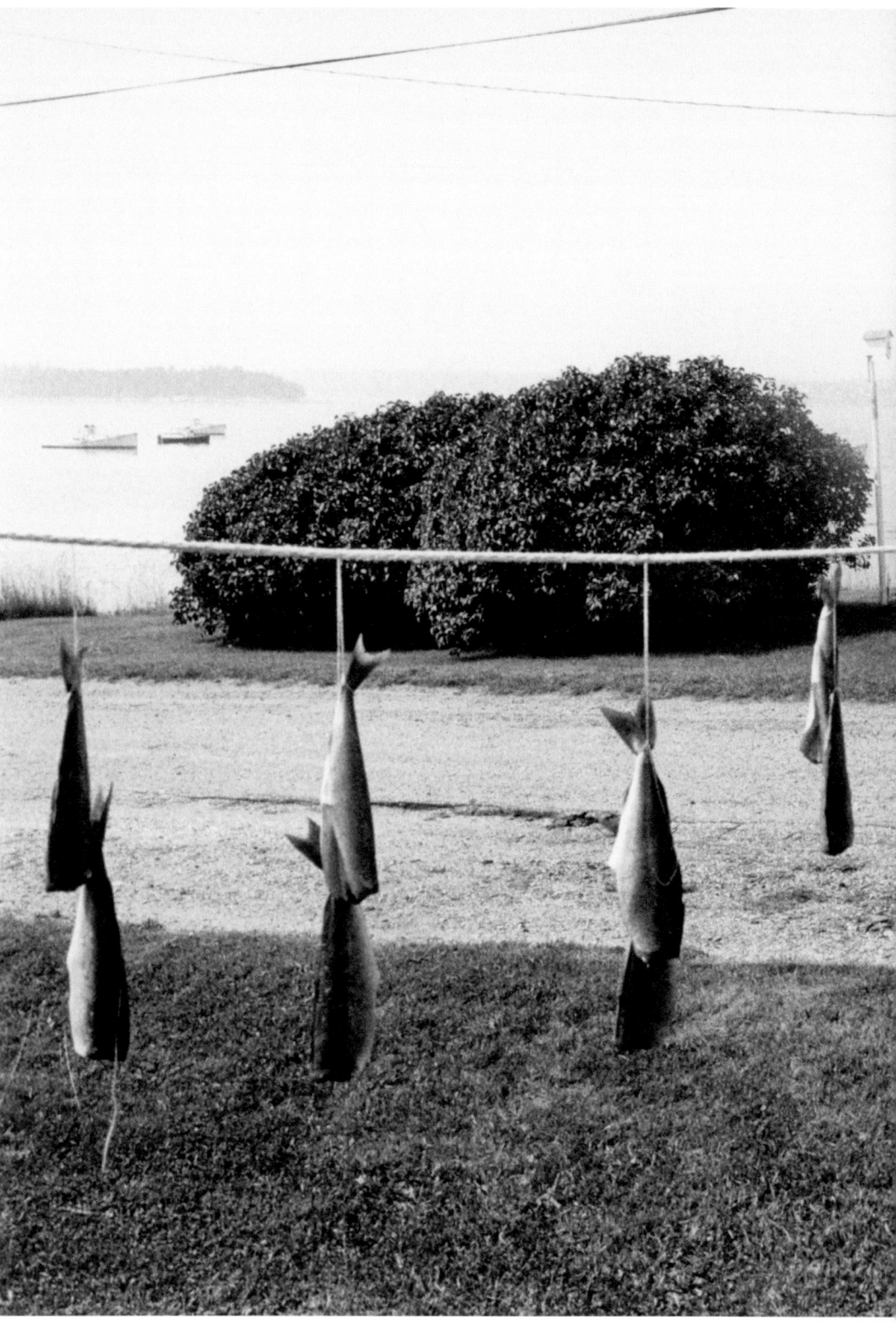

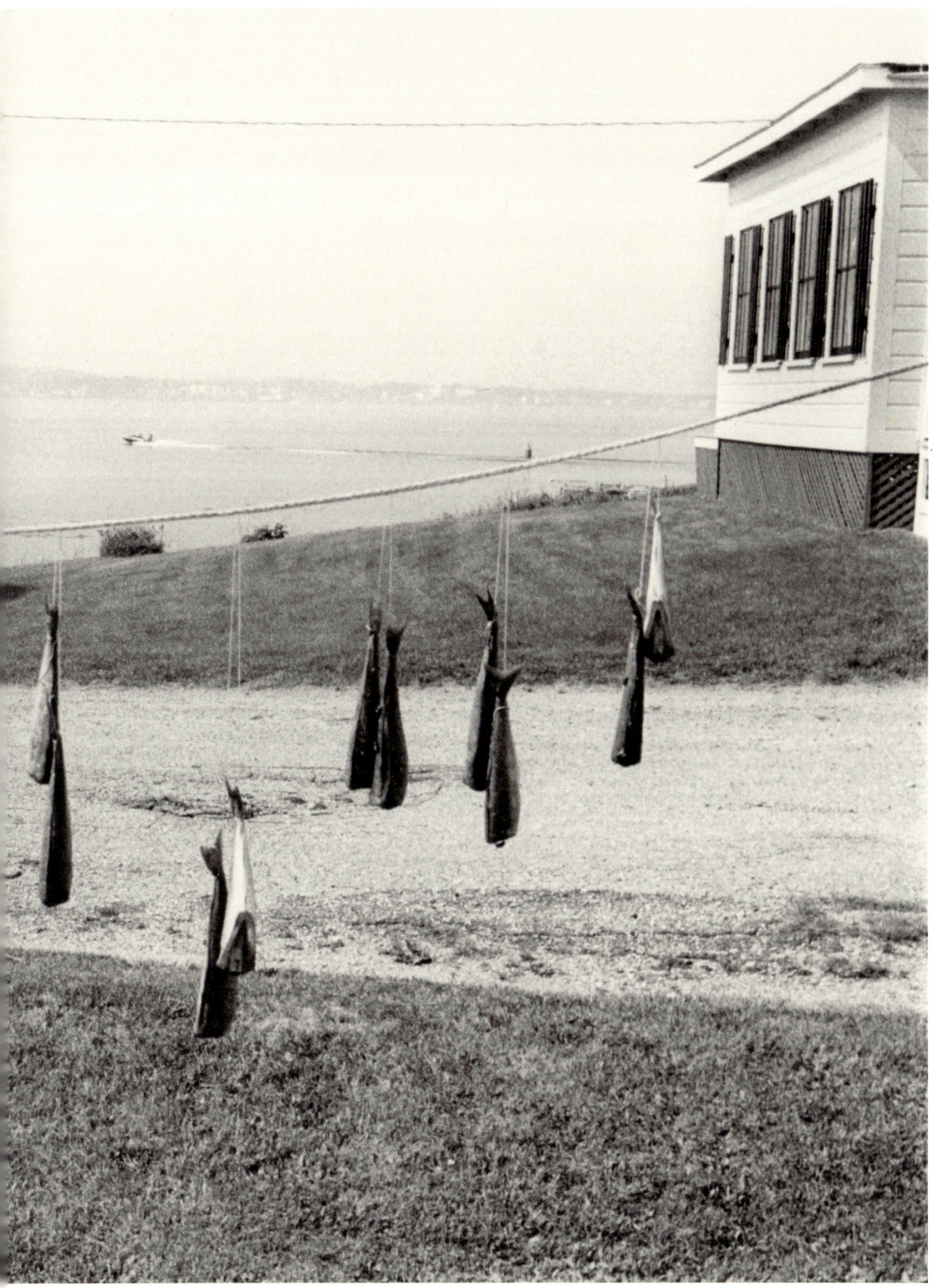

Lotte Jacobi's Baked Potato Pancakes

One of my favorite dishes is "Baked Potato Pancakes" from
The Natural Foods Cookbook by Beatrice Trum Hunter.

From the recipe you know that I am interested in natural foods,
and I am against using sugar, white flour, and chemicals in
my food.

> ¼ cup soy grits
> ¼ cup milk
> 2 cups raw potatoes, grated
> ¼ cup hot milk
> ¾ teaspoon salt
> 1 tablespoon nutritional yeast
> 2 eggs, separated
> 2 tablespoons soy flour

Soak soy grits in ¼ cup milk. Blend potatoes, hot milk, yeast,
and salt. Cool to lukewarm. Add egg yolks, soy flour, and soaked
soy grits. Fold in stiffly beaten egg whites. Pour small
amount of batter onto hot, unoiled soapstone griddle over
moderately high heat. If baked in oven, pour into heated, oiled
pan, and allow 15 minutes at 400 degrees.

Serves 4–6.

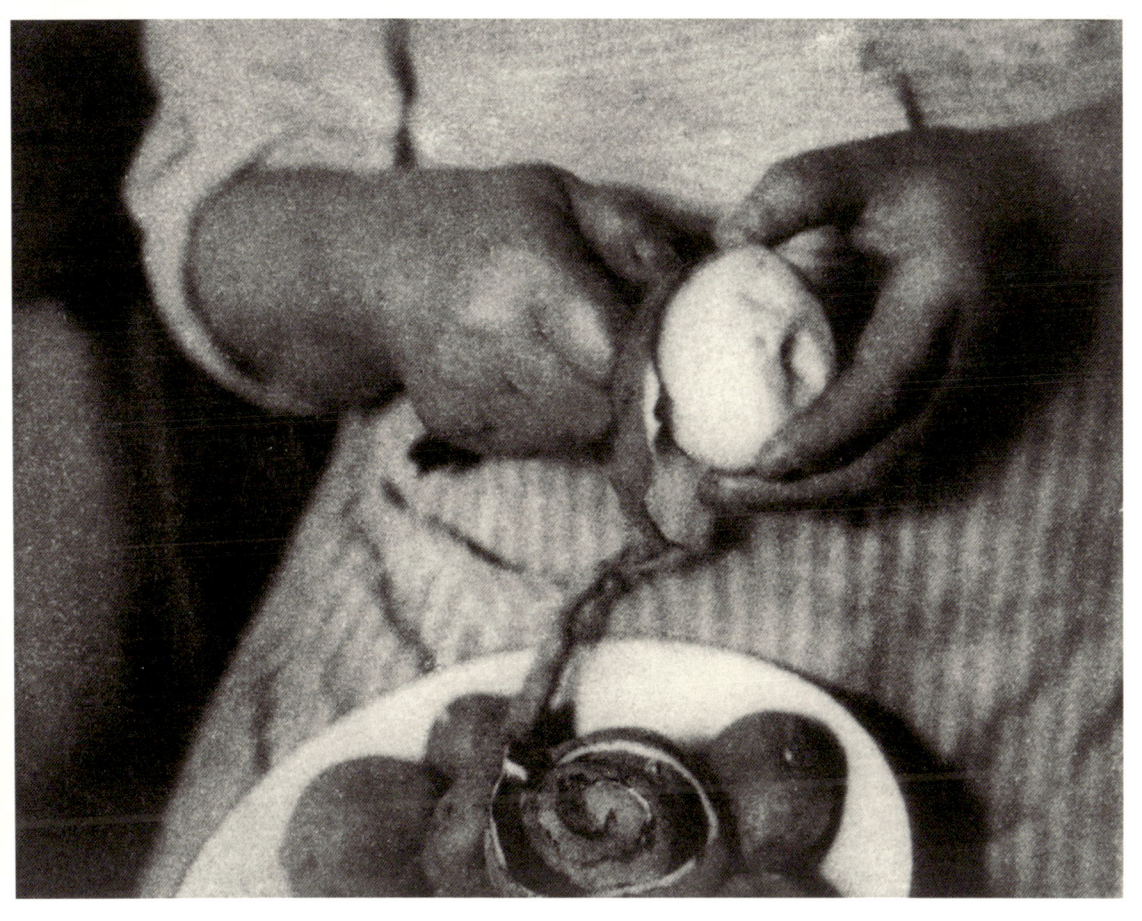

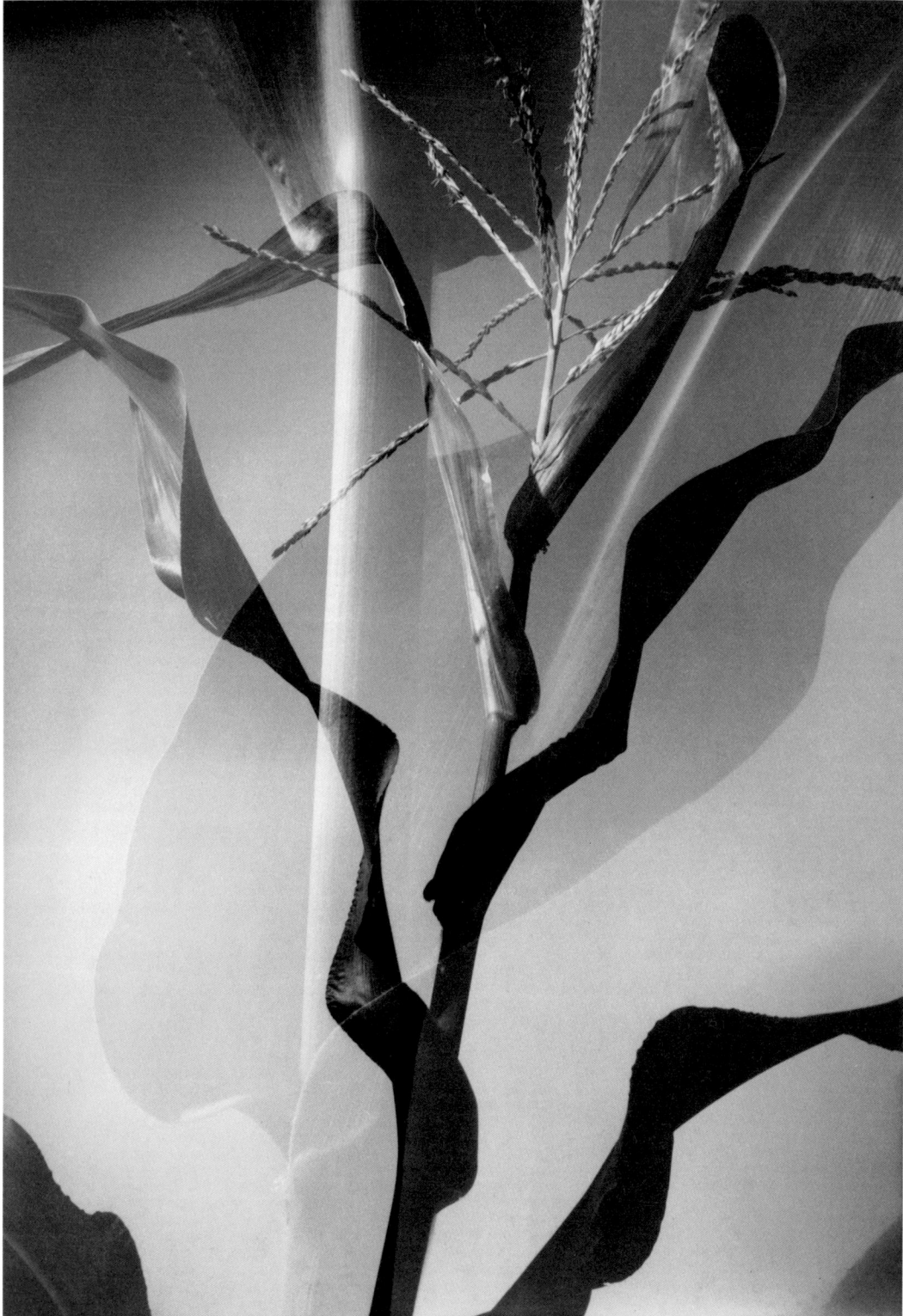

Barbara Morgan's Global Bread Cake

Hoping that we will all someday become "World Citizens,"
I decided to bring some food, originating in other countries, into
a bread-cake mix, such as: soy beans, tapioca, couscous, bananas,
pineapples, cashews, dates, macadamia nuts, etc.

Basically, I was thinking of the grains that keep people alive
around the world: corn, wheat, rye, barley, oats, rice, sesame, soy,
tapioca, buckwheat, taro root, chickpeas, green gram (mung bean);
then raisins, dates, bananas, kumquats, coconut, ginger, lychee
nuts, walnuts, almonds, peanuts, sunflower seeds, pignolis, etc.
I made this as a sort of a UNIVERSAL BREAD idea.

5 cups regular wheat flour
1 cup cooked kernels of corn
2 cups cooked brown rice
1 cup cooked soy beans
1 cup cooked tapioca
1 cup cooked couscous
1 cup cooked millet
1 cup cooked buckwheat
½ cup dried milk
¾ cup corn-oil margarine plus
    melted peanut butter
½ cup raw honey
1½ cups shredded coconut
2 bananas (raw, cut fine)
4 eggs, beaten
¾ teaspoon cinnamon
¾ teaspoon cloves
½ teaspoon ginger

1½ cups pineapples and
    strawberries (cut
    and slightly cooked)
2½ cups almonds,
    walnuts, cashews,
    hazelnuts,
    macadamia nuts,
    pignolis (pine nuts),
    sunflower seeds
    (combined)
1½ cups dates (de-seeded)
    and raisins (seedless)
½ cup peanuts, lychee
    nuts, sesame seeds
    (combined)

111   Barbara Morgan, Corn, Multiple,
      1945

I precooked the grains to retain their character and form, and
then mingled them with the regular wheat flour, which brought
it all together in a spread-out loaf. Then, using nuts, seeds,
dates, and raisins, I added a little mosaic touch as a topping.

This is a first-time experiment; so the balances can, no doubt,
be improved. I did not add water or milk to the mix, for
I kept enough of the fluid from the precooked grains and the
fruit juice.

To be honest, I never "follow recipes." I find it boring and not
enough fun. So I cook according to the weather, the mood of the
people, etc., and try to make it "simple and organic." Apropos
of mood, I remember when I was fascinated by HERBS, that my
son, Lloyd, then 7, had just tasted a new dish we were having
for dinner. He said, "Mother, could we ever eat something that
didn't have a single herb in it?" So then I reformed. But Lloyd
also liked to experiment with fork and spoon, if not with herbs.

Another food idea I live with is to have condiments on the
table in small dishes: coconut, raisins, peanuts, dates, almonds,
soybeans. These vary from day to day. Then people can doctor the
food to satisfy their taste buds as they eat. At one crazy party,
I actually served whale blubber—but only once.

Hans Namuth's French Peasant Bread

1 teaspoon sugar
2 cakes of fresh yeast (2 ounces each)
4 cups warm water (115 degrees)
About 4½ pounds unbleached white flour (divided)
½ cup wheat germ
1 cup yogurt
2 tablespoons honey
4 tablespoons coarse (or kosher) salt
¼ cup olive oil
2 egg yolks, beaten
Cornmeal
Sesame seeds

My favorite bread recipe, changed often over the years, but finally straightjacketed into a simple formula, is called "French Peasant Bread" by some, and "Hans Namuth's Bread" by others. It is usually baked on weekends and gets better as the weather gets hotter. Four loaves—nearly 5 pounds of flour—means a huge amount of dough to be kneaded and is therefore more popular with men. It freezes easily and well. All ingredients should be at room temperature or warmer.

Dissolve sugar and yeast in 115-degree water in a warm bowl. Let stand for 20 minutes or until it bubbles (after stirring it gently). Put most of the flour (but not all—leave 1 pound in the 5-pound bag until you need it) plus wheat germ, yogurt, honey, and salt in a large wooden bowl, and stir with wooden spoon until thoroughly mixed. Start kneading inside your bowl, or, if your bowl is not big enough, on a slightly floured countertop. We assume that you know how to knead. If the dough feels sticky, add flour from your "reserve." When dough is kneaded (5–10 minutes or more), return it to the bowl, sprinkle lightly with flour, cover with a kitchen towel, and put away in an absolutely draft-free, warm place, and let rise until doubled in size. (One hour? Two? It depends on the time of year, the temperature of your house, etc.)

Beat down your dough a second time, and let rise again. After that, repeat the procedure. Then cut the dough into 4 equal parts and shape into round or long loaves—I usually do 2 each. A round bread is prettier, but the long one is easier to slice.

Prepare 2 baking sheets, covering them with wax paper or foil (I prefer the latter), and sprinkling them generously with cornmeal. Two loaves per baking sheet; sprinkle the loaves with flour, cover with towels, and let rise for a third time.

Preheat oven to 350 degrees for 10 minutes. Only now do you slash each loaf with a razor blade or knife (½ inch deep—change pattern each time for variety). Brush on the olive oil, and then, quickly, the egg yolks; sprinkle on the sesame seeds—and put in oven. I have baked bread in many ovens (always preferring gas ovens) and never found two alike. Normally, I leave the oven at 350 degrees for 60 minutes, turning the pans twice during this time, then raising the temperature to 550 degrees for the last 10 minutes. If the bread is slightly burned at times, so much the better.

I always taste the bread as it comes out of the oven (with a bit of sweet butter, it's wonderful)—and sometimes put it back if it is too moist. Cool the loaves on a rack, bottoms exposed.

Makes 4 loaves.

114 Hans Namuth, <u>American Housewife,</u>
       ca. 1952

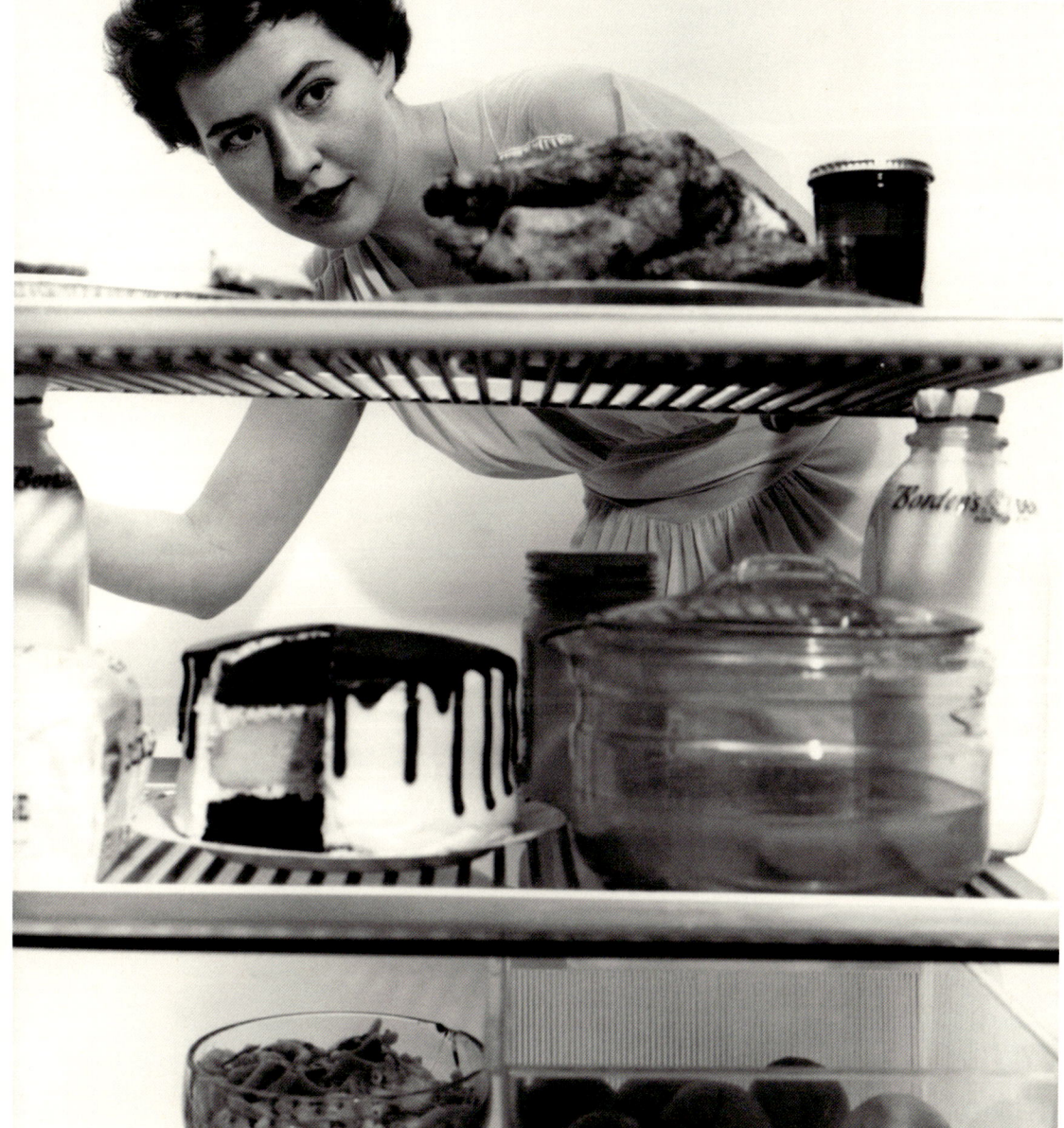

Desserts

Robert Adams: Mom Borland's Big Sugar Cookies

  4 cups flour
  2 cups sugar
  1 cup shortening
  ½ teaspoon salt

Mix the above ingredients as for a piecrust. Then make a well
in the mix and place the following in the well:

  3 eggs
  1 teaspoon vanilla
  1 teaspoon baking soda dissolved in 1 tablespoon water

Mix. Let stand in refrigerator until cool, and then roll out on
a well-floured board. Make large cookies for best results. Bake at
375 degrees for about 15 minutes on an ungreased cookie sheet.

Optional (to make a chocolate "frosting"): After cookies have
baked for 13 minutes, remove cookie sheet from oven, place about
5 chocolate chips in the center of each cookie, return to oven
for 2 minutes, and remove cookies from oven. Swirl the chocolate
with a knife to "frost" each cookie.

118   Robert Adams, Kerstin and Mrs. Leslie Ross, on the Ross
      Wheat Farm, near Peetz, Colorado, 1973

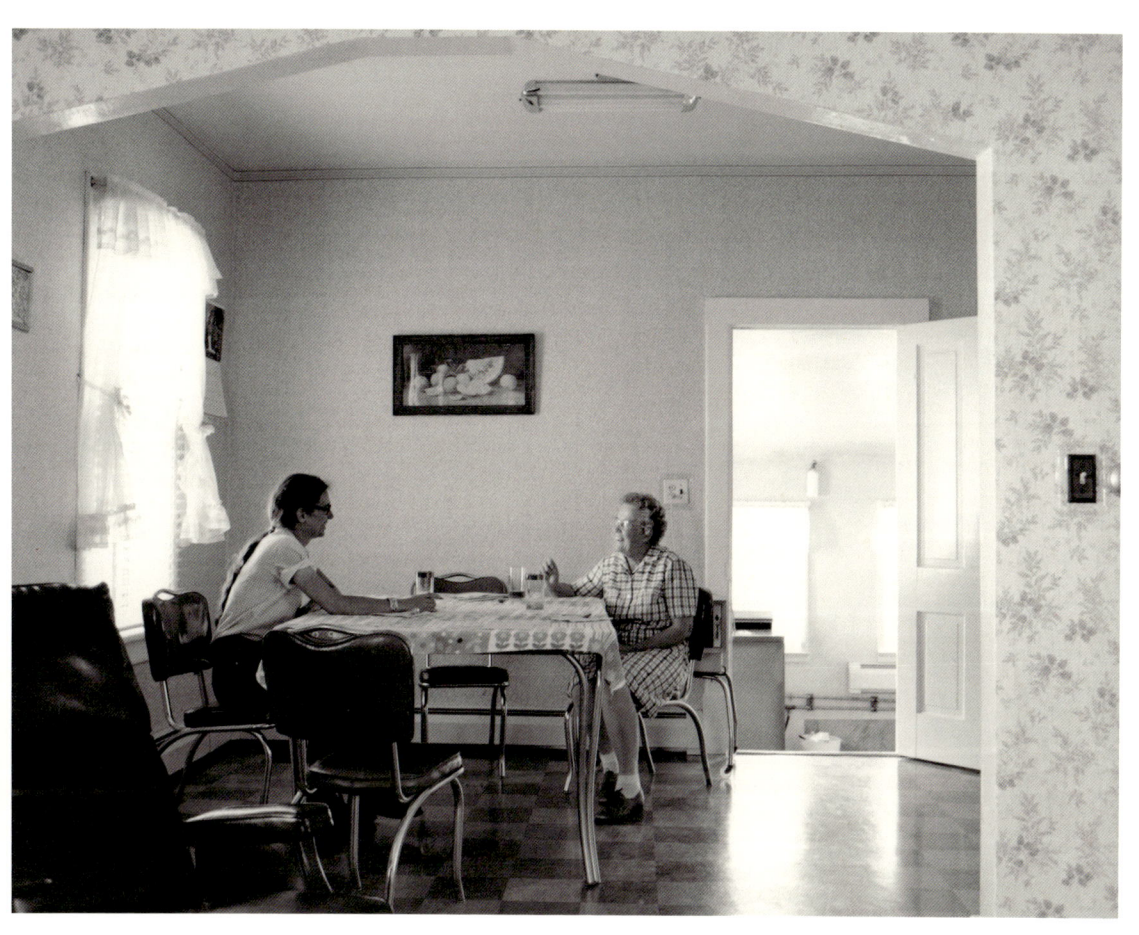

Jim Alinder: The World's Best Brownies

As a complete devotee of chocolate, I have devoured every possible form of that unsurpassed substance. This recipe for brownies— usually considered a somewhat better than average way of eating chocolate—is truly "world class."

Melt 3 squares of unsweetened chocolate with 1 stick of butter. Set aside. Blend 1½ cups sugar and 2 eggs. Add the chocolate mixture, then ½ cup sifted flour. Finally add 1 teaspoon vanilla. Bake in a greased pan 30–40 minutes at 350 degrees. Do not overcook as they must be fudgy. Options include walnuts on top or dusting with powdered sugar.

The Presto Whip is an option best enjoyed in the photograph.

120   Jim Alinder, <u>Big Cans</u>, 1971

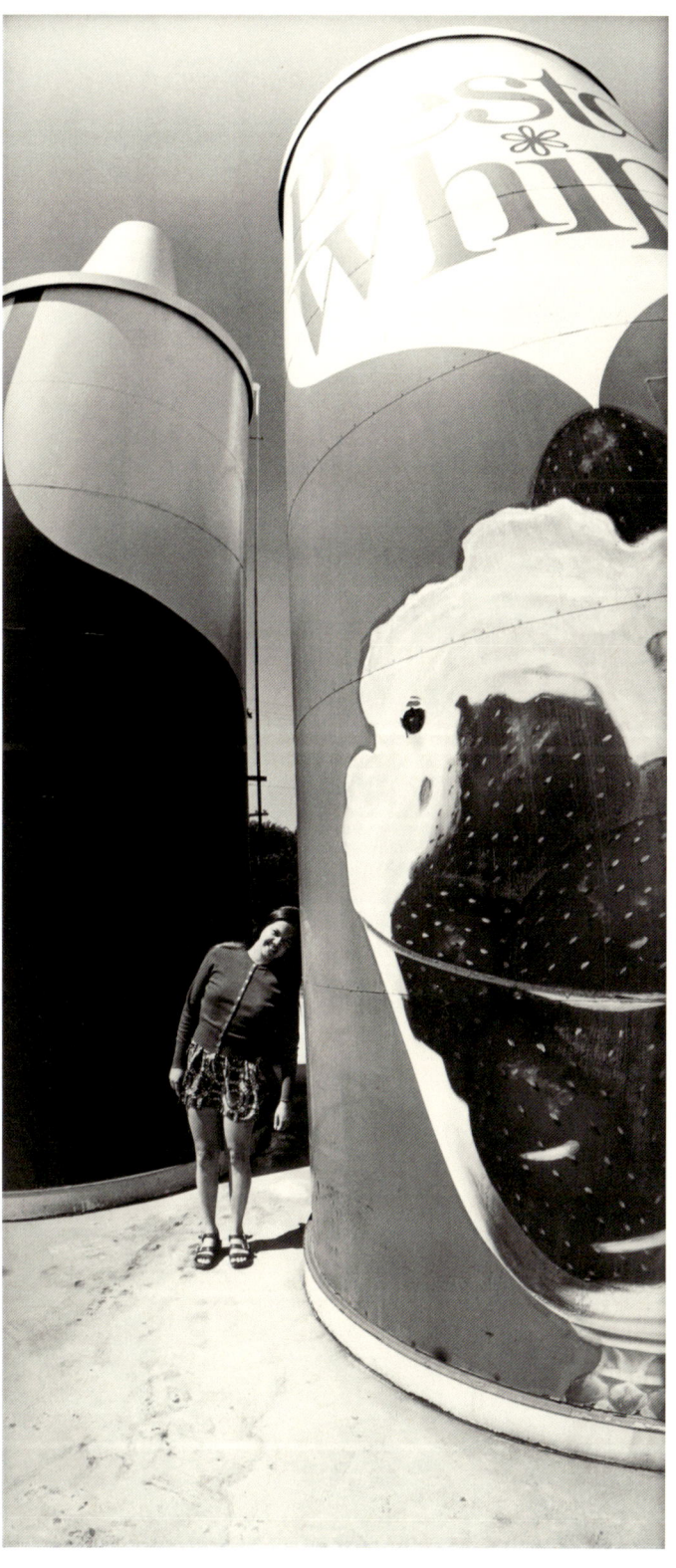

Barbara Crane's Cheesecake

I really love to eat as long as someone else cooks it. I especially love cheesecake.

> 1 graham cracker crust (can use premade)
> 12 ounces cream cheese
> 1 cup cottage cheese
> ¾ cup sugar
> 1 teaspoon vanilla
> ⅛ teaspoon ground nutmeg
> 2 eggs
> ¼ teaspoon ground cinnamon
> 1 can (21 ounces) cherry pie filling

1) Combine 3 packages of the cream cheese with 1 cup cottage cheese, and mix with electric mixer until smooth; beat in sugar, vanilla, and nutmeg. Add eggs, one at a time, beating well after each; measure out ⅓ cup of the mixture and set aside. Pour remaining cheese mixture into the crust.

2) Bake for 30 minutes at 350 degrees. While the cake is baking, take the reserved cheese mixture and the remaining package of cream cheese and mix in a bowl; beat until smooth. Take a pastry bag with round tip and fill with the mixture. You will use this mixture to decorate the cake. Add the ground cinnamon to the cherry pie filling.

3)   Remove the cheesecake from the oven at the end of
      30 minutes. Increase oven temperature to 450. Spread the
      cherry filling (with cinnamon added to it) over cheesecake.
      Take pastry bag (filled with reserved cheesecake mixture)
      and decorate the top. Bake decorated cheesecake in
      hot oven (450) for 10 minutes or till the top decoration
      is browned. Cool completely on wire rack.

Serve at room temperature.

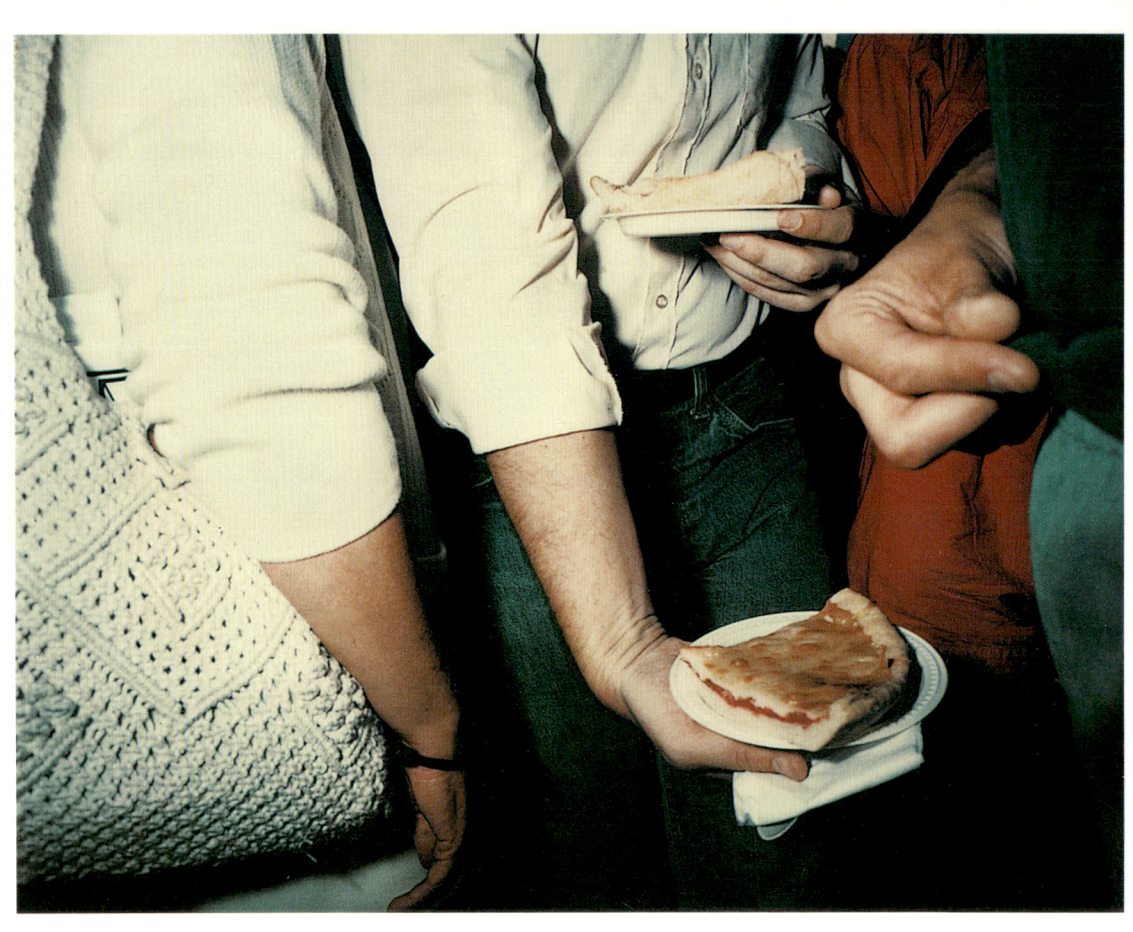

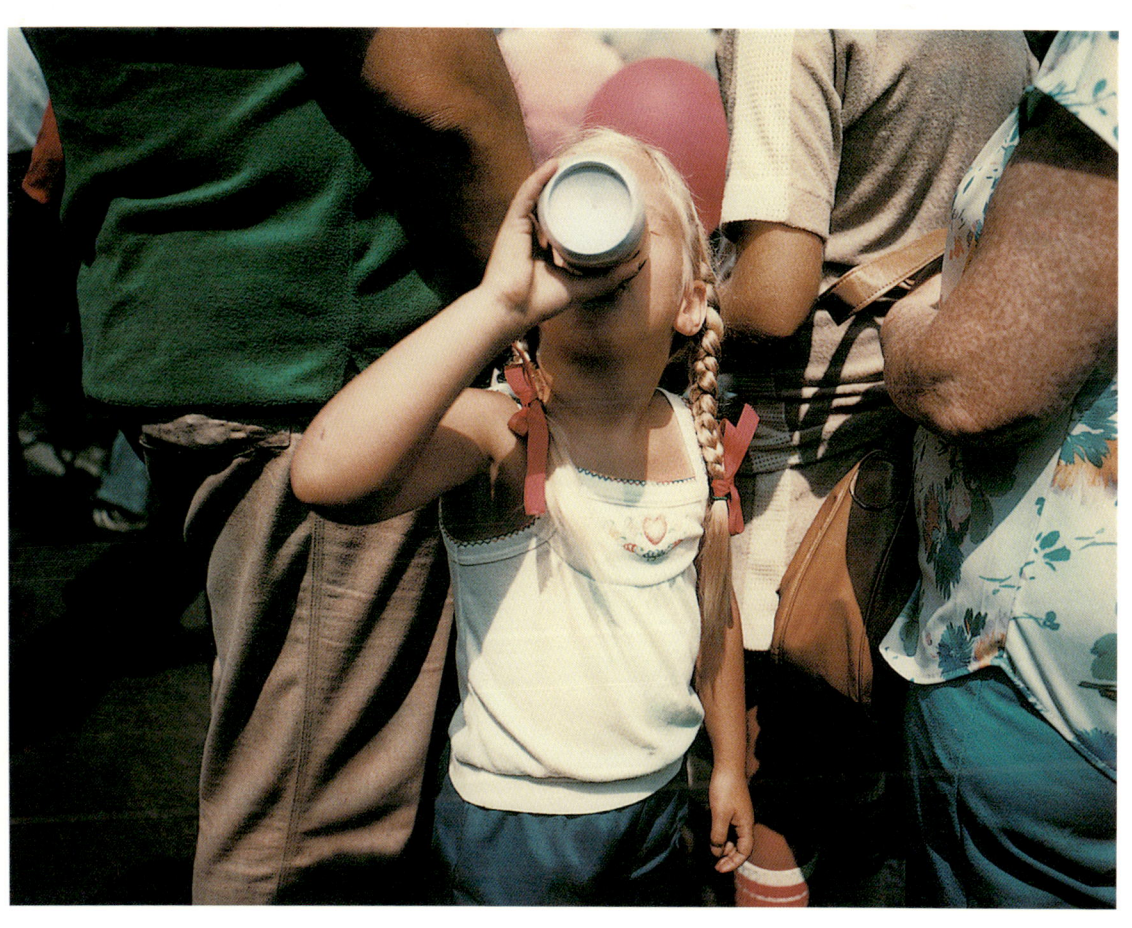

Jack Delano's Puerto Rican–Style Coffee

The photograph is part of my coverage of a Thanksgiving dinner with the Crouch family in Ledyard, Connecticut, in 1940, for the Farm Security Administration.

Many years later I realized that the only thing missing from this sumptuous meal was the kind of coffee I now enjoy here every day. Puerto Rican coffee, now available in many Hispanic communities in the United States, is not a blend but pure, finely ground coffee beans grown in our highlands. It is, for me, the only proper way to begin a day or end a meal.

It is prepared by using 1 heaping tablespoon of coffee (ground Puerto Rican–style) to 1 cup of water.

Bring water to a boil, and turn off heat.

Add coffee to water.

Stir for a few moments and pour the mixture through a filter. (Never boil!)

Many people like it with hot milk, but I take mine black, with sugar.

126 Jack Delano, Pumpkin Pies and Thanksgiving Dinner at the Home of Mr. Timothy Levy Crouch, a Rogerine Quaker Living in Ledyard, Connecticut, 1940

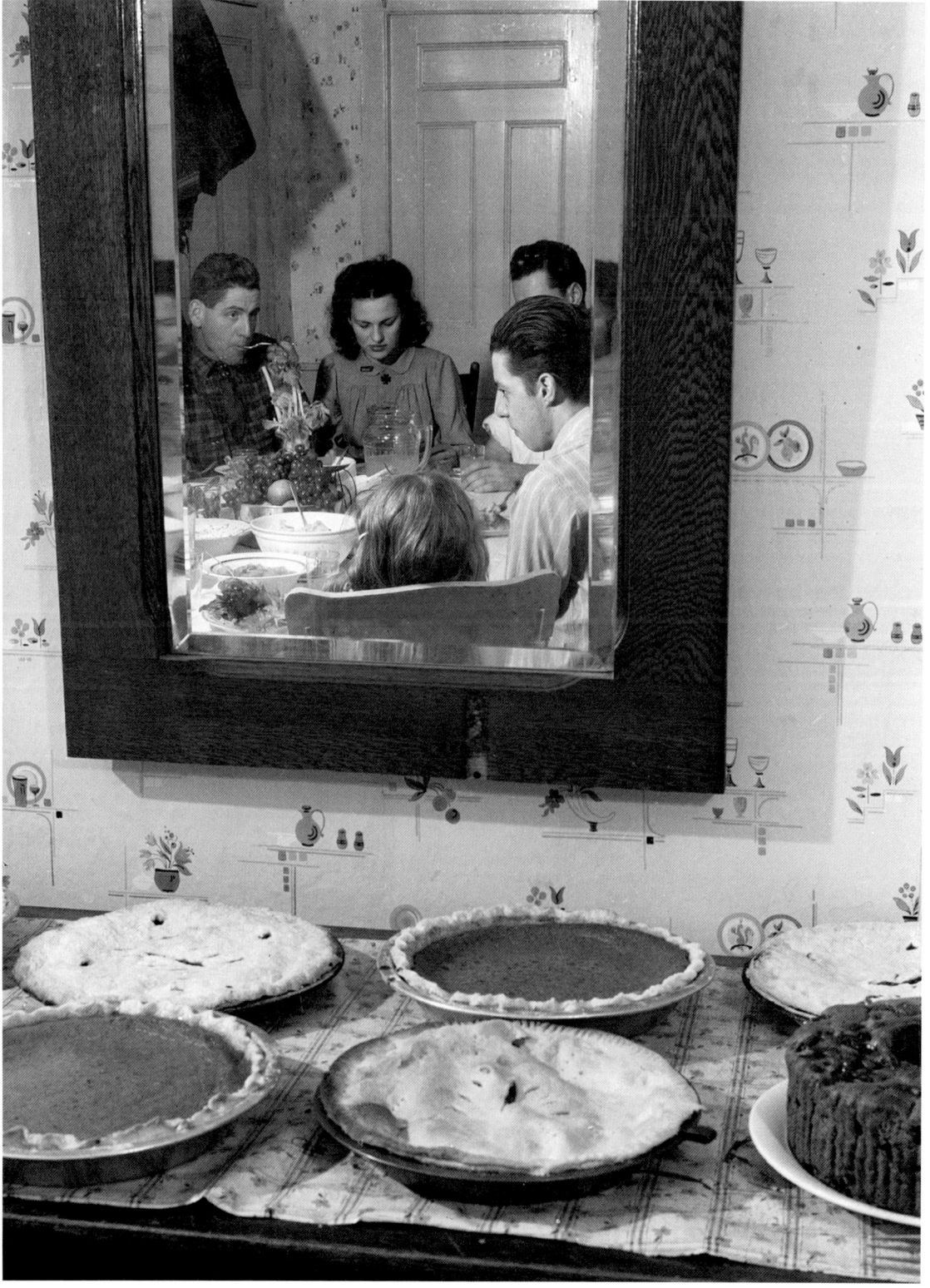

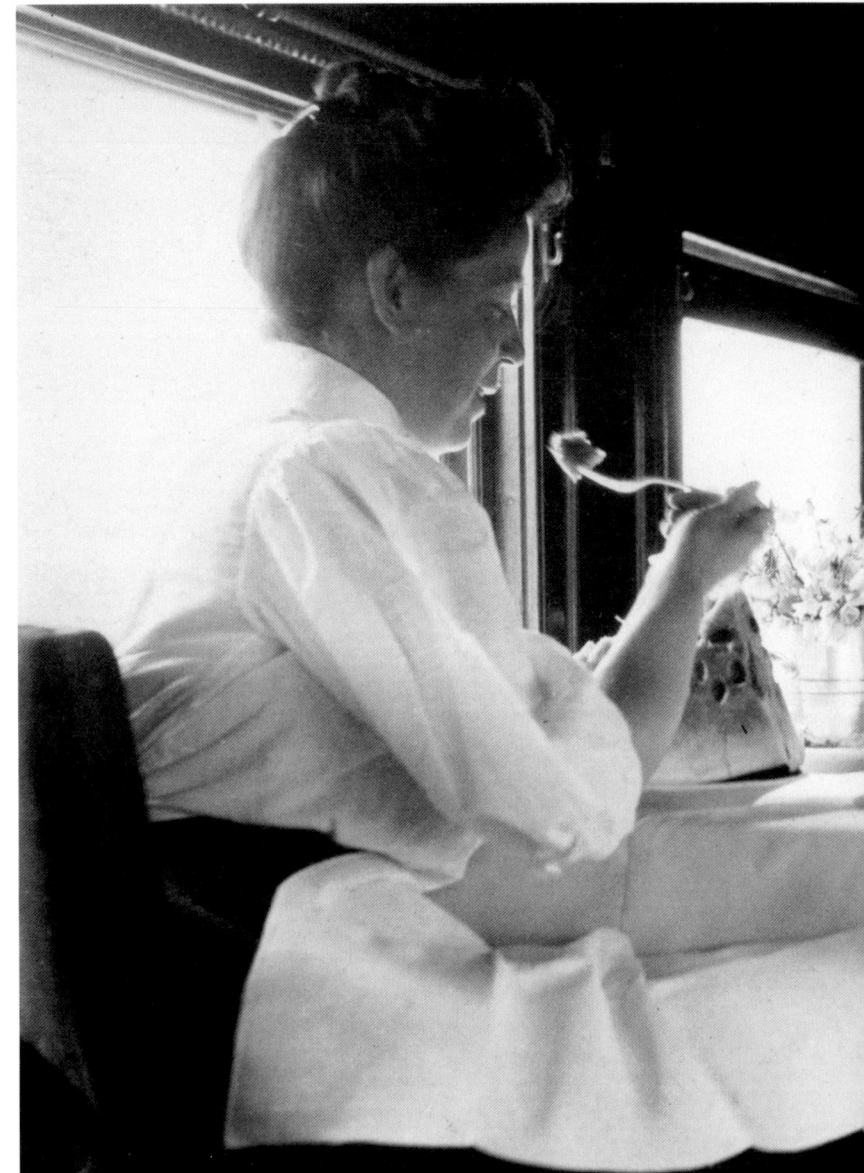

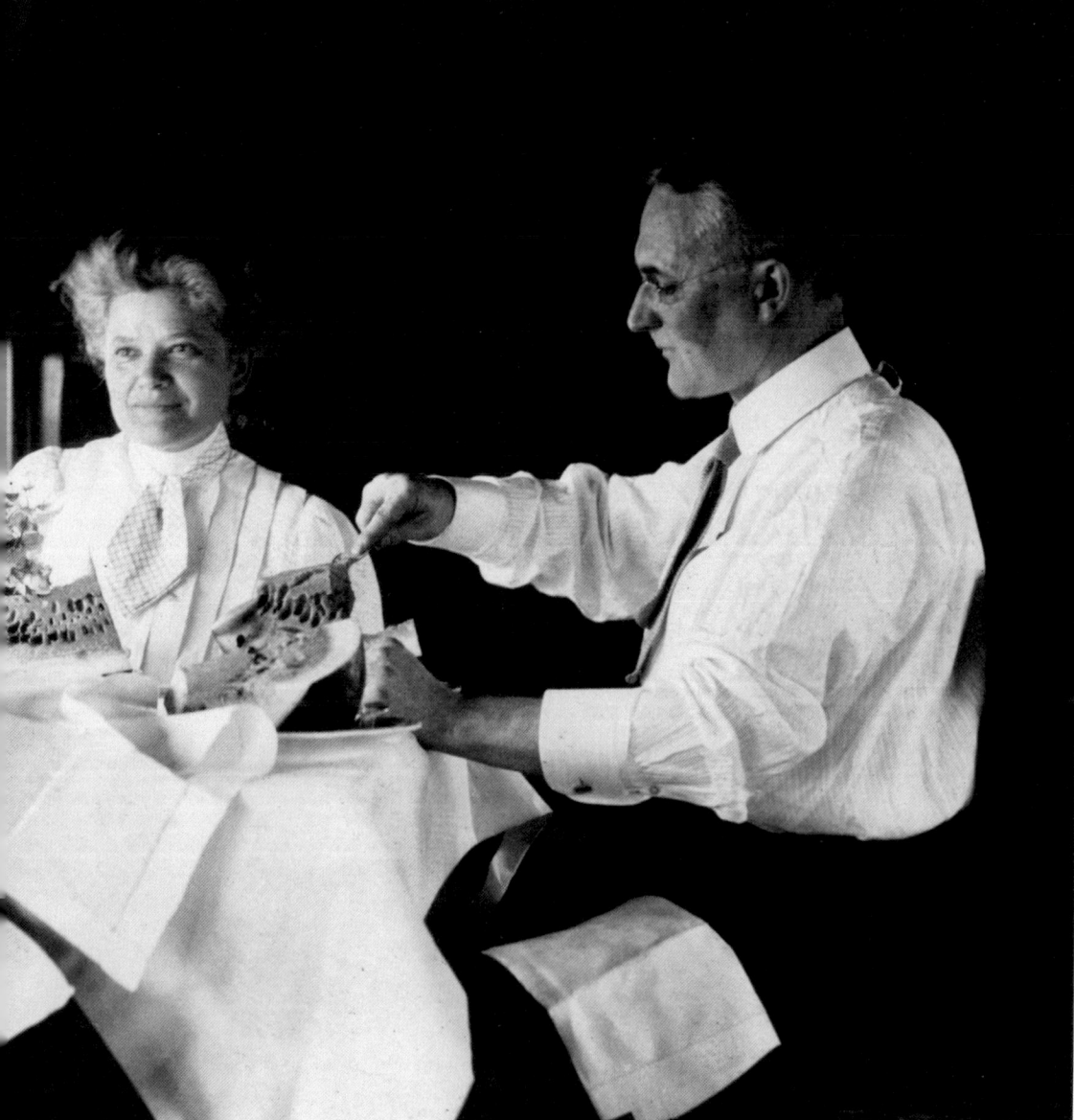

George Eastman's Lemon Meringue Pie

6 eggs (separated)
1 cup granulated sugar
2 lemons

Beat yolks of 6 eggs with 1 cup of granulated sugar. Add grated rind and juice of 2 lemons. Cook 15 minutes in double boiler, stirring constantly. Take from fire and when cool, add the beaten whites of 3 eggs.

Crust
1 cup flour
½ cup Crisco
A little salt
½ teaspoon baking powder

Mix crust ingredients till granular, add water to moisten.

Fill crust, which has been baked a light brown.

Make meringue with 3 remaining egg whites. Add 2 tablespoons sugar while beating egg whites, top off and put in oven to brown.

130   Photographer unknown, George Eastman dining with
      Eleanor Eastwood and Josephine Dickman in railroad car,
      Wyoming Trip, 1908

Betty Hahn's Kolacky

This is my favorite recipe. It is pure POLISH.

    1 cup butter or margarine (at room temperature)
    1 package (8 ounces) cream cheese (at room temperature)
    ¼ teaspoon vanilla extract
    2¼ cups all-purpose flour
    ½ teaspoon salt
    Thick jam or canned fruit filling, such as apricot or prune

1) Cream butter and cream cheese until fluffy. Beat in vanilla extract.

2) Combine flour and salt; add in fourths to butter mixture, blending well after each addition. Chill dough until easy to handle.

3) Roll dough to ⅜-inch thickness on a floured surface. Cut out 2-inch circles or other shapes. Place on ungreased baking sheets.

4) Make a "thumbprint" about ¼-inch deep in each cookie. Fill with jam.

5) Bake at 350 degrees for 10–15 minutes, or until delicately browned on edges.

Makes about 3½ dozen.

131 Betty Hahn, Grapefruit, Watermelon, Sweet Potatoes, Eggplant, Rochester, New York, 1971

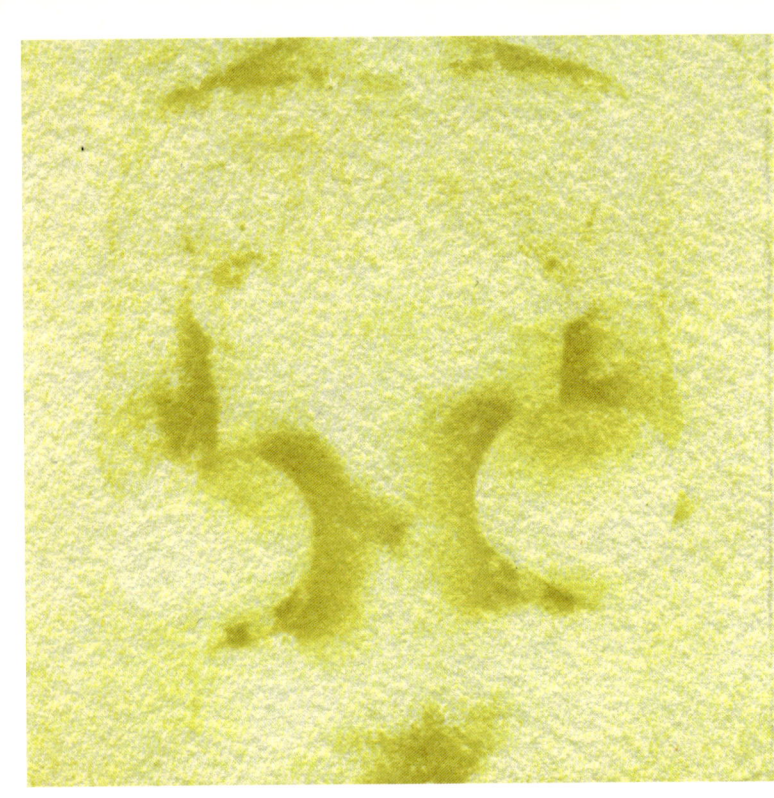

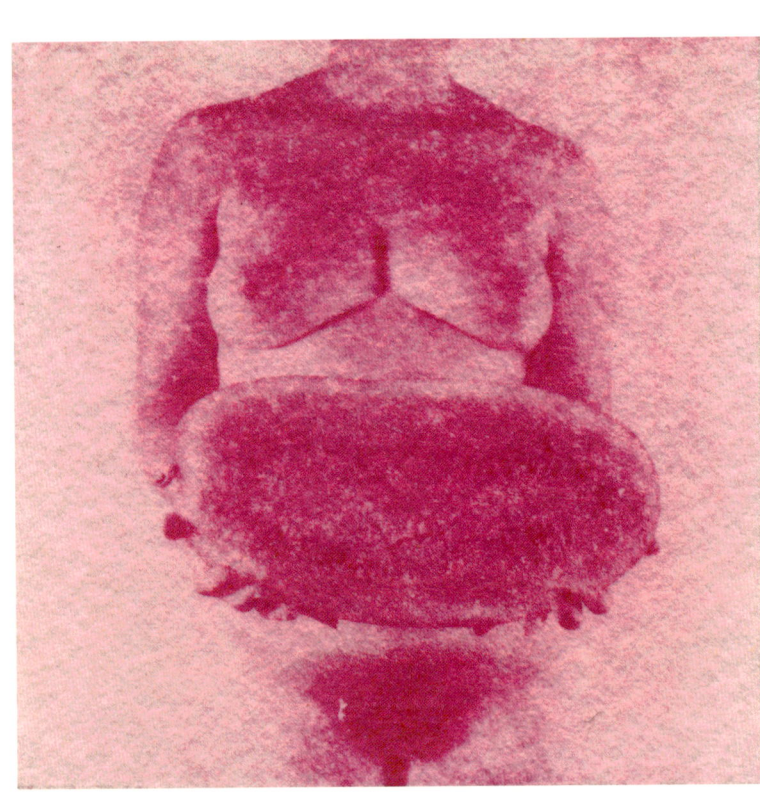

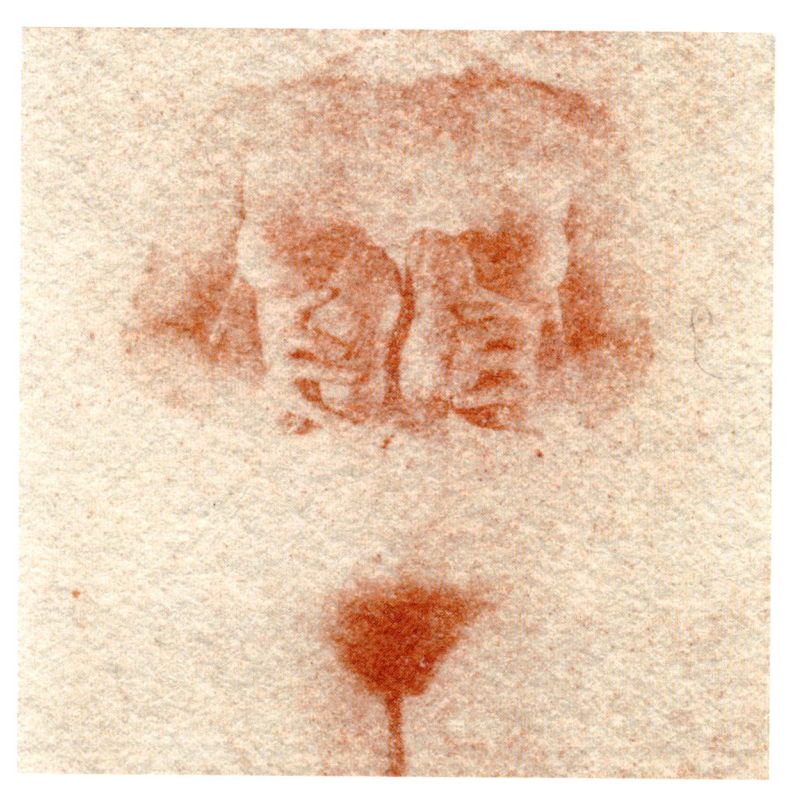

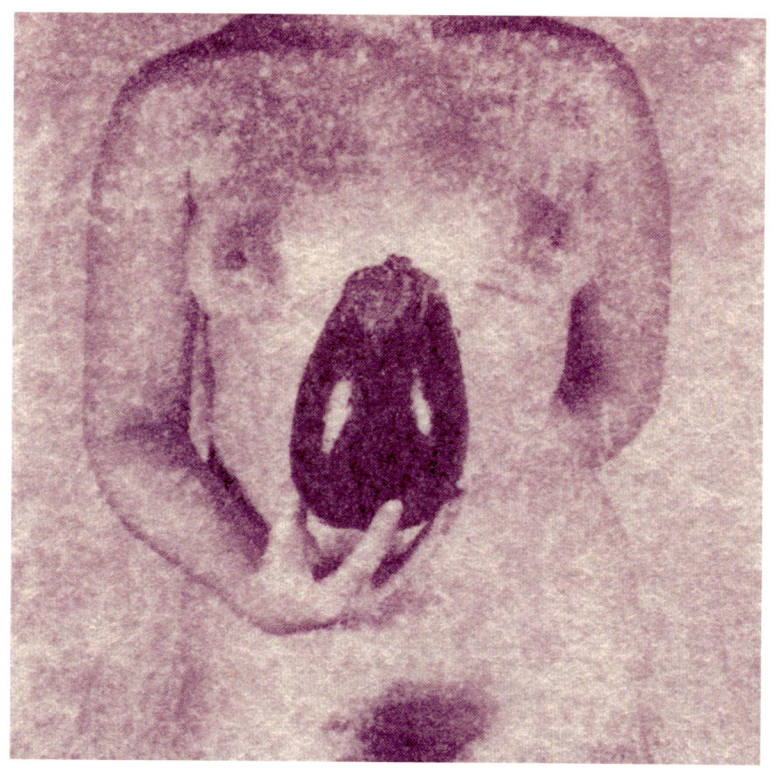

Joseph Jachna's Potato Chip Cookies

Cream together:
    1 pound whipped margarine
        (preferably at room temperature)
    1½ cups sugar
    2 teaspoons vanilla

Mix all together and add to the margarine and sugar mixture:
    3½ cups flour
    1 bag (2½ ounces) potato chips, crushed
    3½ ounces to 1½ cups chopped pecans

Drop by teaspoonful onto ungreased cookie sheet.

Bake 10–12 minutes at 350 degrees on the top rack of the oven.

Dust with powdered sugar when cool.

My wife baked 40–50 dozen of these for my last opening
(University of Illinois, Circle Campus) in Chicago. They were all
devoured and later comments about the success of the opening
affirmed, for me, the connection between these cookies and my
photographs. Also, like potato chips, you can't stop eating 'em!

134   Joseph Jachna, <u>Still Life</u>,
      1968

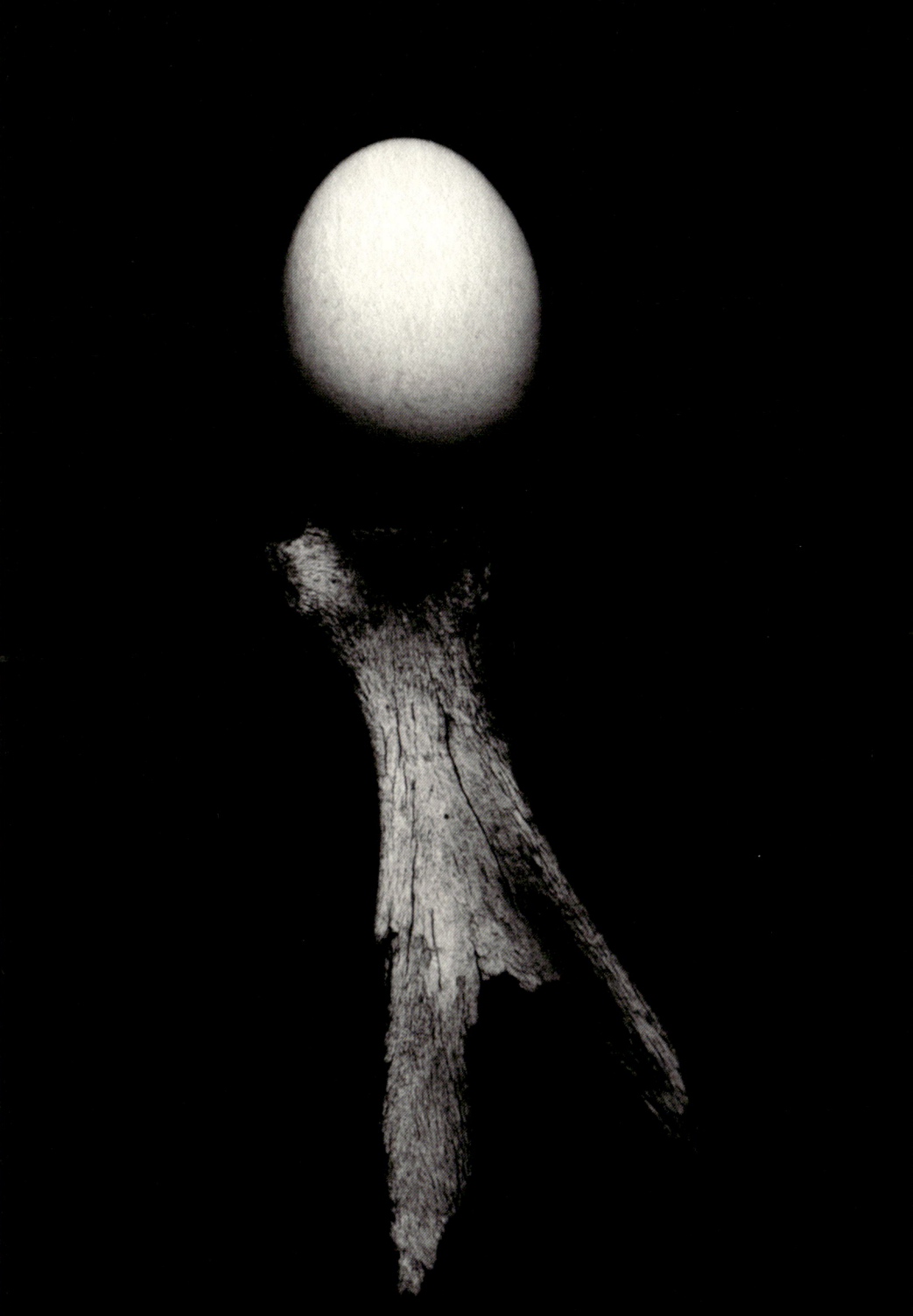

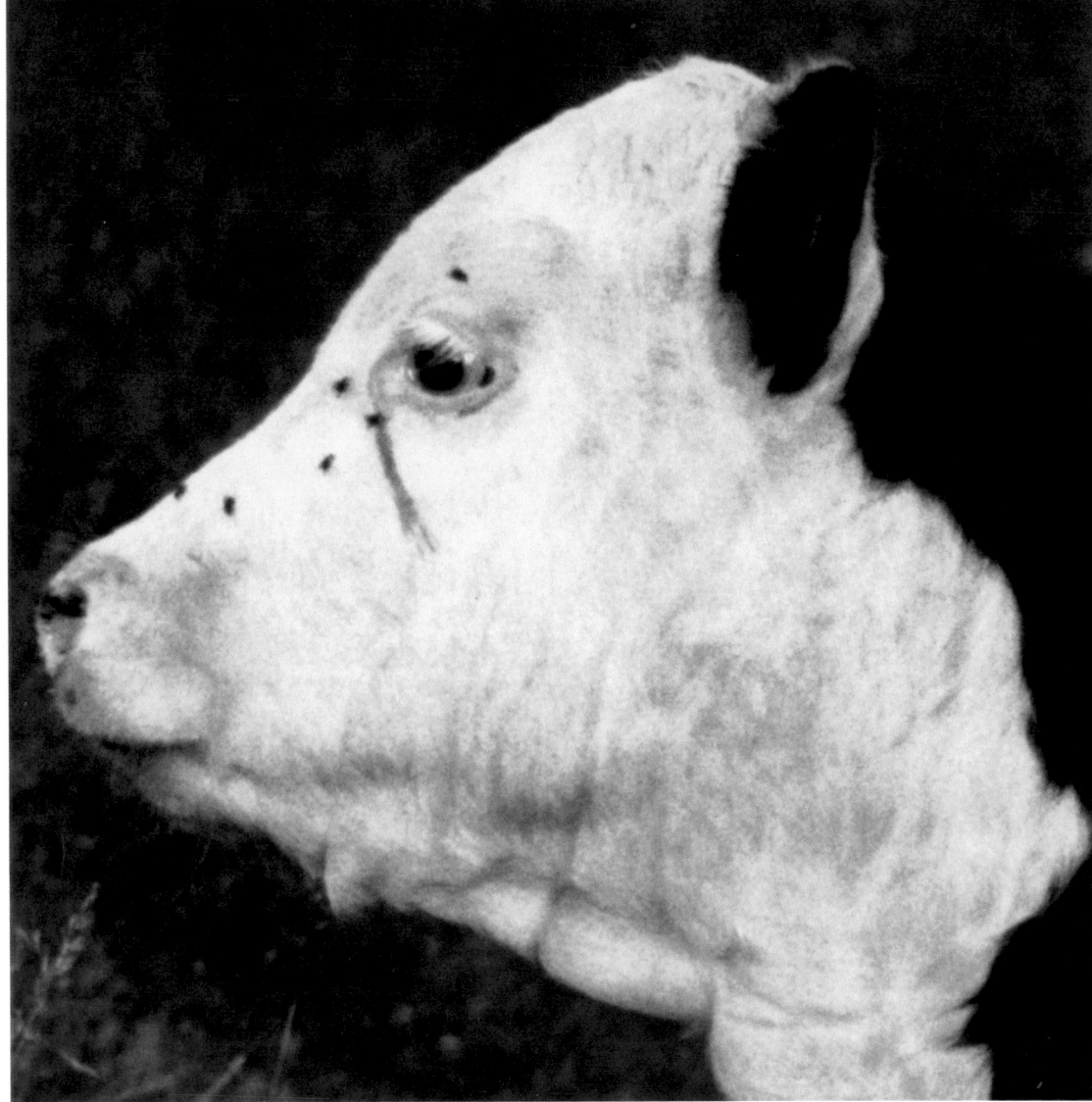

Richard Margolis's Shoofly Pie

2⅓ cups white flour
2 cups firmly packed brown sugar
½ teaspoon cinnamon
⅛ teaspoon cloves
⅛ teaspoon ginger
⅛ teaspoon nutmeg
⅛ teaspoon allspice
⅔ cup melted butter
10 ounces light molasses
⅔ cup hot water
1 teaspoon baking soda
3 (9-inch) pastry shells
Vanilla ice cream (optional)

Mix together the first 7 ingredients. Cut in the melted
butter with a pastry blender or two knives until the mixture
is crumbly. Set aside. Combine the next 3 ingredients and
stir. Divide the liquid into the 3 pie shells and top with the
crumbly mixture. Bake in a preheated oven at 450 degrees
for 10 minutes, then reduce heat to 350 degrees for 20 minutes,
or until firm. It should be eaten warm with vanilla ice cream.

137   Richard Margolis, Penland (After Coburn),
      1978

Grant Mudford's Pavlova

There are many things from Australia I remember with great affection, partly due to their absence elsewhere in the world. I truly miss: Old Holdens (cars), gladioli (flowers), galas and kookaburras (birds), Ayers Rock (natural monument), and the Bush (outback country). Australian cuisine on the whole is forgettable, with one notable exception—the pav!

Named after the famous Russian dancer, Anna Pavlova, who in 1926 performed Swan Lake in Australia, the master chef at a reception in her honor prepared the taste treat Australians now know so well.

Description: a soft marshmallow-centered dessert with crisp and lightly browned meringue crust, topped with fresh whipped cream and fresh fruit.

> Egg whites
> 2 rounded tablespoons of sugar to each egg white—
>   use at least 8 egg whites
> Drop of vinegar to each egg white

Preheat oven to 300 degrees. Beat egg whites until stiff. Add sugar gradually while beating; add vinegar. Prepare an oven tray covered with a piece of greased or wax paper—spread mixture out in a disc shape (about 9 or 10 inches in diameter). Put "Pavlova" in oven, and immediately turn down heat to 225 degrees. Bake for a total of 1½ hours. Toppings, as suggested (see note below) should be added just before serving (the base wrapped in plastic wrap will keep 7–10 days in a cool, dry place; weeks in the refrigerator).

Toppings: whipped cream topped with strawberries, pineapple, cherries, kiwi fruit, and other fresh fruits are suggested.

138   Grant Mudford, Untitled,
      1978

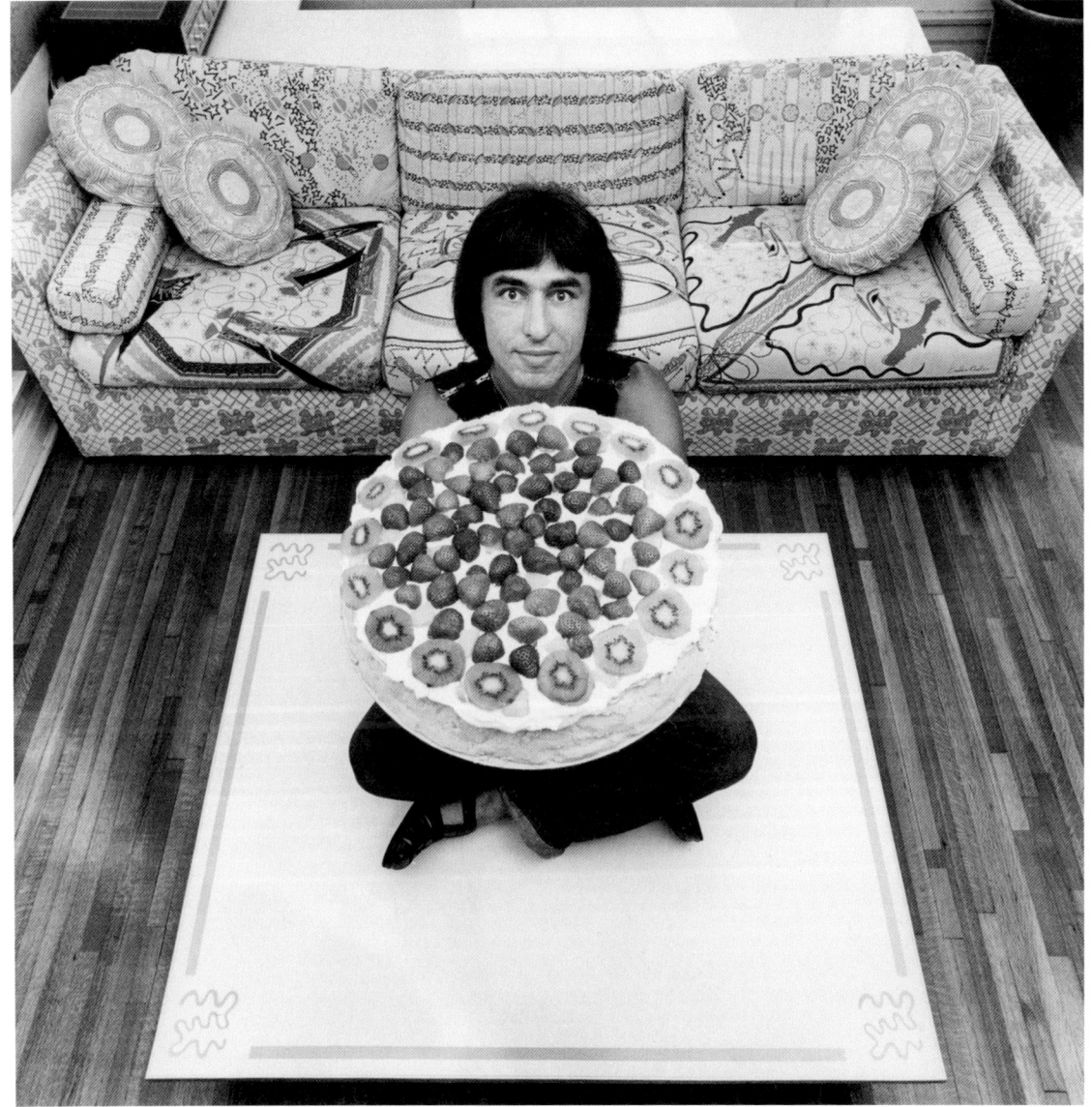

Stephen Shore's Key Lime Pie Supreme

Crust

Make graham cracker crust following instructions on box, but increasing all the quantities 50 percent. Be sure to use brown sugar.

Filling

1 cup sugar
¼ cup flour
3 tablespoons cornstarch
¼ teaspoon salt
2 cups water
3 egg yolks
1 tablespoon butter
Juice of 2 large limes (approximately ⅓ to ½ cup)
Grated rind of 2 limes
1 container of heavy whipping cream

1) Combine sugar, flour, cornstarch, and salt in a saucepan, and stir in water gradually. Cook on medium heat until thickened. Add the beaten egg yolks gradually and return to a low heat, and cook for 2 minutes, stirring constantly.

2) Stir in the butter, lime juice, and rind and allow them to cool slightly. Pour into the baked pastry shell and cool.

Topping

Make whipped cream with 1 container of heavy whipping cream and sweeten with sugar.

140 Stephen Shore, New York City, New York,
September–October 1972

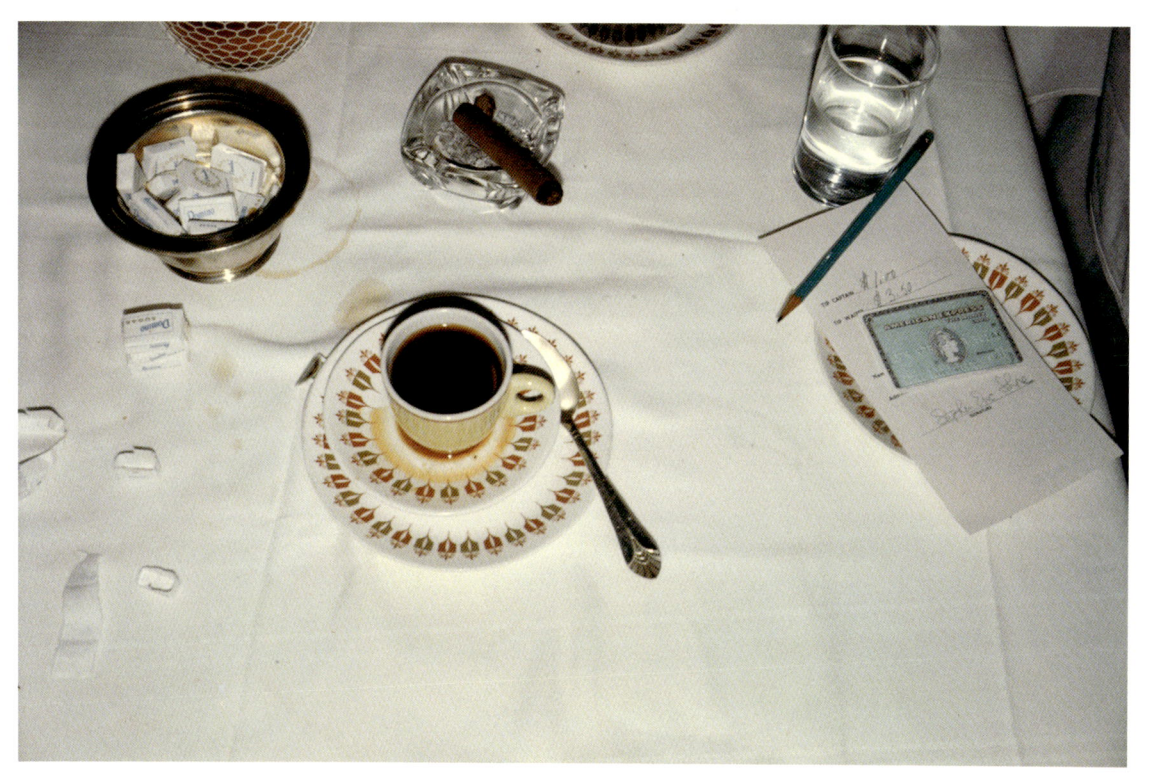

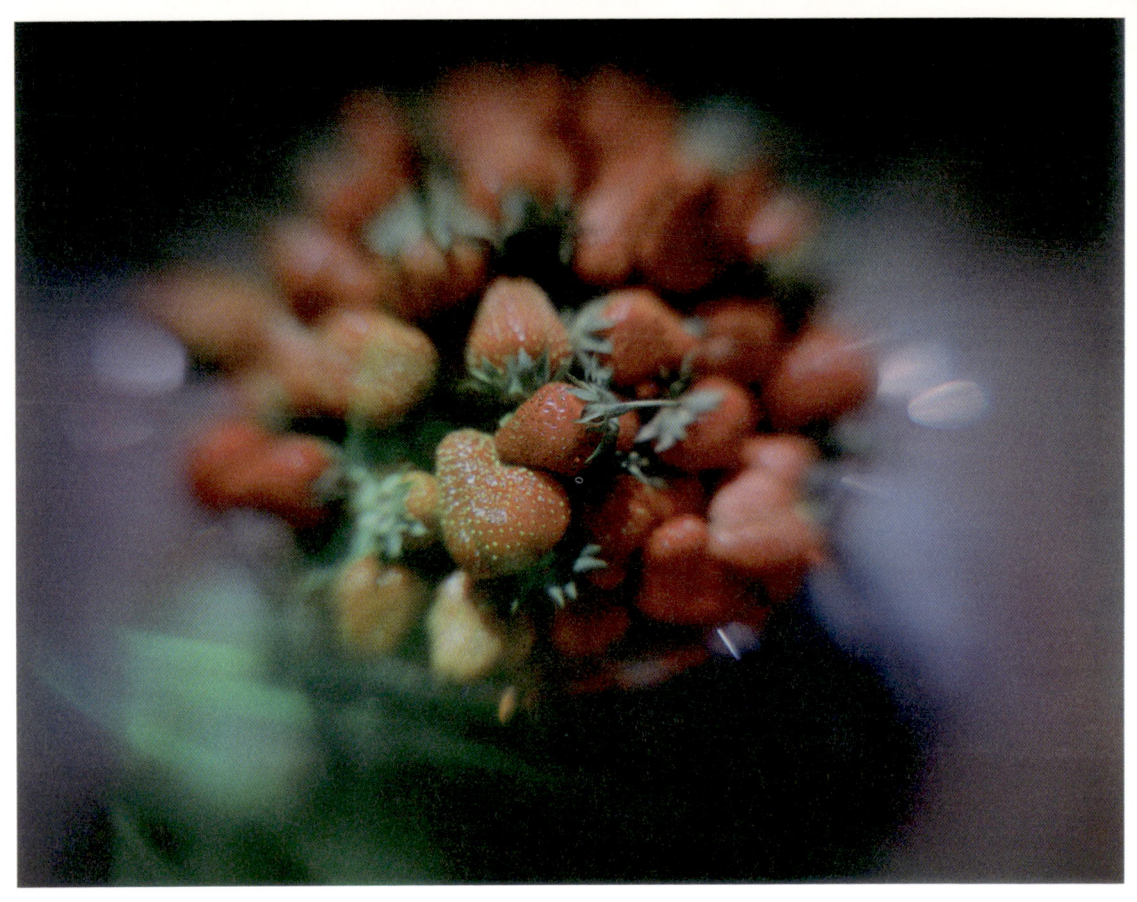

Charles Swedlund's Strawberry Pie

Made by Liz Swedlund, enjoyed immensely by Charles Swedlund.

One of the things I like most about this part of the country
[Illinois] is having fresh strawberries in May and June.
At 30 cents a pound (U-Pick), strawberries find their way
into every meal. For these two months we live on strawberries
—only seems natural that they also make their way into
my photographs.

> 1 baked pie shell
> About a quart of strawberries (divided)
> 1 cup water (divided)
> 1 cup sugar
> 3 tablespoons cornstarch
> Whipped cream or ice cream (optional)

Directions:

> Wash, drain, and hull strawberries. Simmer 1 cup
> strawberries and ⅔ cup water about 3 minutes. Blend
> sugar, cornstarch, and remaining ⅓ cup water; add to
> boiling mixture. Boil 1 minute, stirring constantly. Cool.
> Place remaining strawberries in pie shell (save a few
> pretty ones). Cover with cooked mixture and garnish
> with the choice berries. Refrigerate until firm—about
> 2 hours. Serve with plenty of whipped cream or ice
> cream—it is even good by itself!!!!

143 Charles Swedlund, Strawberries,
     1979

Drinks

Robert Heinecken's Serious Martini

English gin
California lemon

1) Take one bottle of either Tanqueray or Bombay gin.
Beefeater should not be a substitute.

2) Take long-stem crystal glass, preferably with straight
v-shaped sides, minimum capacity 3 ounces.

3) Place both in freezer, 5–6 hours prior to intended imbibing.

4) For each serving, pour the desired amount (minimum
3 ounces) directly from the bottle into frozen glass.
Use no ice, and avoid touching the bowl of the glass.

5) Add the juice of ⅛ California lemon. Remove any seeds and
submerge the lemon slice rind in the drink.

6) Serve and repeat for maximum effect.

Note A. An excellent companion to this drink is iced shrimp
dipped to taste in cocktail sauce with lemon juice added.

Note B. This drink is not recommended before 11:00 a.m.

146   Robert Heinecken, PP/Whiskey—Figures/E,
1991

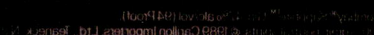

Mark Klett's Home-Brew Beer

While most of us are familiar with the commercially available carbonated malt beverage known as "beer," few have experienced the pleasure of the carefully made "home-brew." During Prohibition the art of home beer-making was given a bad name by those who exercised sloppy technique or used inadequate equipment. Today, brewing has been scientifically researched and made safe and simple for basement brew masters. All ingredients and equipment are available from winemakers supply stores and will concoct a drink of exceptional flavor and potency. While, technically, home beer-making is still illegal, many amateur winemakers have switched to beer-making because of its relative ease, faster rate of production, and flavor which is superior to domestic beers.

The recipe below is one which I have found particularly successful. The result is a form of "steam beer," or beer which ferments around the temperature of 65 degrees and a variety that I find as good as "lager" beer (lager beers ferment at approximately 38 degrees and take longer to mature).

Equipment:

    1 unused plastic garbage pail and lid
        (at least 5-gallon capacity)
    1 (5-gallon) water bottle (such as used in water coolers)
    1 air lock top (for 5-gallon water bottle)
    1 bottle capper and bottle caps
    2 cases crown type (i.e., returnable) beer bottles

Ingredients:

    1 (3-pound, 8 ounces) can Munton & Fison
        un-hopped light malt extract
    4 cups corn sugar (do not use white sugar)
    1 Superbrau beer yeast pack
    1 Hallertauer powdered hops package (same hops used
        in Heineken beer)
    5 gallons cold water
        (use hard water, unchlorinated, if possible)

Procedure:

1)   Boil 1 gallon of water in saucepan. Add can of malt extract
    and 4 cups corn sugar. Stir ingredients until dissolved,
    then add hops. Boil mixture for 10 minutes.

2)   Put 3 ½ gallons cold water in clean plastic garbage pail and
    add the hot mixture of water, malt, and corn sugar to it.
    After stirring, add beer yeast. Cover garbage pail with lid
    and place in a cool, dark place. Fermentation will now take
    place and a layer of foam will form on top of the liquid.

3)   When the foam subsides (1–2 days), transfer the liquid
     (green beer) into the 5-gallon water bottle and attach
     air lock. Allow to ferment in this container 5–7 days or
     until the beer becomes clear and stops bubbling.

4)   Siphon the beer back into the clean garbage pail, leaving
     sediment behind. Add 1 cup of corn sugar to 1 quart of the
     beer in a saucepan. Boil, and dissolve the sugar in the beer;
     add the mixture to the rest of the beer. Bottle and cap the
     beer using the beer bottles. Age it at room temperature
     for at least 2 weeks. Peak flavor is reached in 35 days, and
     the beer will last indefinitely. A small amount of
     sediment will form on the bottoms of the bottles, and the
     beer should be poured carefully into a mug for drinking.
     This sediment is yeast and is not harmful, and is also
     delicious when used in bread-making.

150   Mark Klett, <u>Tea Break at Teapot Rock,</u>
      1997

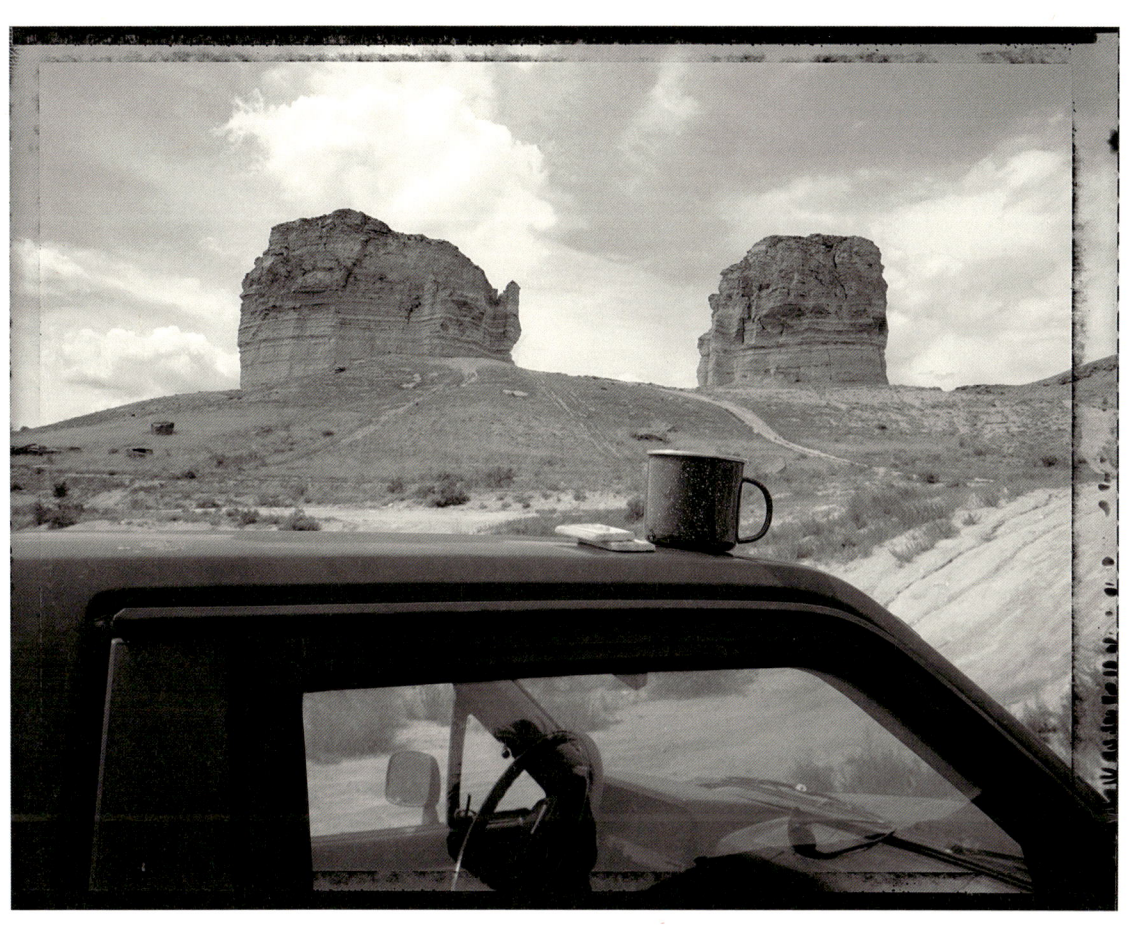

153

Image credits

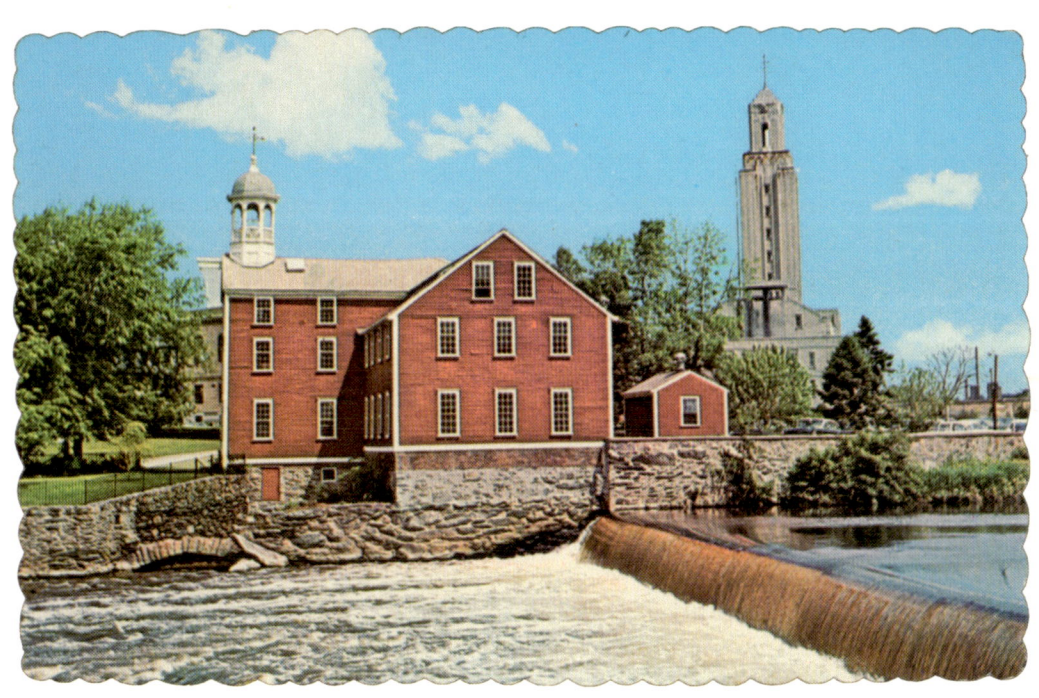

157   Postcard from Harry Callahan, submitted to
The Photographer's Cookbook, 1978

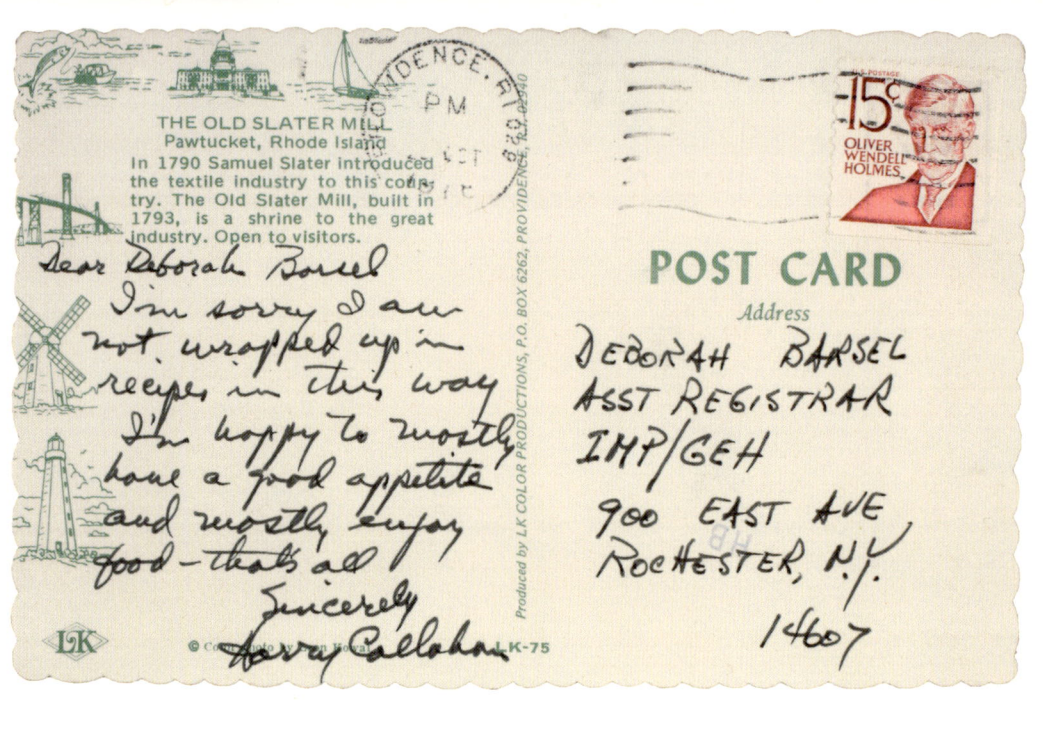

THE OLD SLATER MILL
Pawtucket, Rhode Island
In 1790 Samuel Slater introduced
the textile industry to this country. The Old Slater Mill, built in
1793, is a shrine to the great
industry. Open to visitors.

Dear Deborah Barsel
I'm sorry I am
not wrapped up in
recipes in this way
I'm happy to mostly
have a good appetite
and mostly enjoy
food—that's all
Sincerely
Harry Callahan

Produced by LK COLOR PRODUCTIONS, P.O. BOX 6262, PROVIDENCE, R.I. 02940

LK

LK-75

POST CARD

Address

DEBORAH BARSEL
ASST REGISTRAR
IMP/GEH
900 EAST AVE
ROCHESTER, N.Y.
14607

15¢
OLIVER
WENDELL
HOLMES

Acknowledgments

This book would not exist without Deborah Barsel.
Her imagination and hard work in the 1970s were its genesis,
and her kindness and generosity in 2015 were critical to its
realization. We are deeply grateful to her.

Our colleagues at Aperture and at the George Eastman Museum
were also instrumental to the creation of this book. Our thanks
go to Jonathan Knight Newhall, Robyn Taylor, Nicole Moulaison,
Thomas Bollier, David Arkin, William Green, Ross Knapper,
Elizabeth Chiang, Sarah Evans, Barbara Galasso, and Sheila
Foster. We also acknowledge the editorial efforts of copy editor
Catherine Field, and thank Sonya Dyakova and Charlotte Hauser
of Atelier Dyakova for the book's fresh design. Thank you also
to Julia Turshen for her advice and enthusiasm. Two former
members of the George Eastman Museum's staff, Sean Corcoran
(now curator of prints and photographs at the Museum of the
City of New York) and Jessica Johnston (now assistant director
and curator of collections at Visual Studies Workshop), deserve
recognition as well for their rediscovery and advocacy of
The Photographer's Cookbook.

Finally, our sincere thanks to all the photographers—those who
responded to Deborah Barsel in the 1970s as well as those
who answered our inquiries forty years later. Your participation
in this project has allowed us to understand photography,
photographers, and community in new and fascinating ways.

Thank you.

—

Lisa Hostetler
Curator in Charge, Department of Photography
George Eastman Museum

Denise Wolff
Senior Editor
Aperture Foundation

The Photographer's Cookbook
Originally conceived and edited
by Deborah Barsel
Introduction by Lisa Hostetler

Front cover: Beaumont Newhall,
Edward Weston's Kitchen, 1940
Back cover: William Eggleston, Untitled,
1976; from the series Election Eve

Editor: Denise Wolff
Design: Atelier Dyakova
Production Director: Nicole Moulaison
Production Manager: Thomas Bollier
Assistant Editor: Jonathan Knight Newhall
Copy Editor: Catherine Field
Senior Text Editor: Susan Ciccotti
Proofreader: Madeline Coleman
Work Scholars: David Arkin, Sophie Klafter,
Cassidy Paul

Additional staff of the Aperture book program
includes: Chris Boot, Executive Director;
Sarah McNear, Deputy Director; Lesley A.
Martin, Creative Director; Kellie McLaughlin,
Director of Sales and Marketing; Amelia Lang,
Managing Editor; Samantha Marlow, Assistant
Editor; Katie Clifford, Project Editor and
Executive Assistant; Taia Kwinter, Assistant
to the Managing Editor

The Photographer's Cookbook is copublished
with the George Eastman Museum in
Rochester, New York.

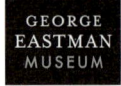

GEORGE
EASTMAN
MUSEUM

First edition
Printed in China
10 9 8 7 6 5 4 3 2 1

Library of Congress Control Number:
2015953488
ISBN 978-1-59711-357-1

Aperture Foundation books are distributed
in the U.S. and Canada by:
ARTBOOK | D.A.P.
155 Sixth Avenue, 2nd Floor
New York, N.Y. 10013
Phone: (212) 627-1999
Fax: (212) 627-9484
E-mail: orders@dapinc.com
www.artbook.com

Aperture Foundation books are distributed
worldwide, excluding the U.S. and Canada, by:
Thames & Hudson Ltd.
181A High Holborn
London WC1V 7QX
United Kingdom
Phone: + 44 20 7845 5000
Fax: + 44 20 7845 5055
E-mail: sales@thameshudson.co.uk
www.thamesandhudson.com

aperture

Aperture Foundation
547 West 27th Street, 4th Floor
New York, N.Y. 10001
www.aperture.org

Aperture, a not-for-profit foundation,
connects the photo community and its
audiences with the most inspiring work,
the sharpest ideas, and with each other
—in print, in person, and online.